O BRAVE NEW CHUR

O BRAVE NEW CHURCH

Rescuing the addictive culture

MARK STIBBE

DARTON · LONGMAN + TODD

First published in 1995 by
Darton, Longman and Todd Ltd
1 Spencer Court
140–142 Wandsworth High Street
London SW18 4JJ

ISBN 0–232–52054–2

A catalogue record for this book is available
from the British Library

Unless otherwise stated the scriptural quotations are taken
from the New International Version of the Bible published by
Hodder and Stoughton Ltd.

Extracts from *Brave New World* by Aldous Huxley
are used by permission of Random House UK Ltd.

Phototypeset in 11/14pt Bembo by Intype, London
Printed and bound in Great Britain by
Redwood Books, Trowbridge

This book is dedicated to our first child,
Philip Giles Stibbe

Contents

Preface

This has not been an easy book to write. There are two main problems that a Christian confronts when undertaking any major project about the addictive nature of society. First of all, the subject of addiction can itself become addictive. I have, during the course of my research, read several books and met several people whose words have suggested to me that they have become excessively attached to the concept of addiction. The idea of addiction can, for some people, become as 'mood-altering' as any fix: that danger lies before anyone who tackles this issue. Let the reader beware.

Secondly, the actual study of society's addictions is perhaps one of the most depressing areas of research we can grapple with. Investigating the gloomy, furtive world of the sex addict, or the drug addict – or pretty well any kind of addict – leaves a grey cloud of depression over you which can easily affect your own spirituality. In terms of spiritual warfare, we must understand that penetrating the world of addiction is a move into enemy territory. If we are not careful, we can easily become tainted and polluted by what we find there. Again, let the reader beware.

On a more positive note, however, I am bound to say that this line of investigation is essential to the Church's mission today. Many of the people whom the Church is trying to win for Christ are actually addicted. In order to attract them, we must therefore address issues of addictive

lifestyles. When they become Christians (which is happening in large numbers at the moment), we must help
them to find healing from the inner wounds that triggered
the cycle of addiction in the first place. In my own church
here in Sheffield, I have seen first-hand the beautiful
healing work of the Lord Jesus Christ in the lives of
addicted people. Some who were close to losing their
sanity, their marriages, their jobs, have been given a
wholeness and a joy beyond their dreams. That has been
a work of grace, and it has been marvellous in our eyes.
So whilst addictionology may be a dark and difficult
subject, there are great rewards for those who want to
apply insights from it in the practical ministry of their
churches. I hope very much that *O Brave New Church*
proves helpful to you.

Acknowledgements

When a book has been a struggle to write there are bound to have been supportive people in the background. I would like to pay tribute to these.

First and foremost, I want to acknowledge the help of Morag Reeve at Darton, Longman & Todd. She has been very understanding when the pressures both of parish ministry and of the project itself became, for a while, too much. Her willingness to postpone the delivery date has been greatly appreciated, not just by me but by my family.

Secondly, I owe a debt to those who have a similar interest in the addictive society. Father Mike Crosby, whose books on Matthew's gospel from an addiction-ological perspective are well known, is one such friend and colleague. When Mike and I first met we found that iron really does sharpen iron. We fed off each other's ideas and developed a keen sense of intellectual affinity. Another person to whom I am grateful is Don Williams of the Vineyard Church. It was his leaders' day back in 1991, at St Thomas' Crookes, which first indicated to me the importance of 'addiction' for the understanding of our culture. I owe a deep debt to Don.

Thirdly, I want to thank my friend Tim Smithies, the Diocesan Youth Officer in the Sheffield Diocese. Tim has been my companion at movies, amusement arcades, consumer electronics shows and many other venues besides. Researching popular culture with a Christian brother has been essential, especially on the rare occasions

when I felt it necessary to investigate some of the more
seamy aspects of the mass media. His support, advice and
help has been instrumental in the completion of this
project.

Fourthly, I want to thank Margaret Wadsworth.
Margaret – a member of our church here in Grenoside –
has been keeping her eye on the newspapers and sending
me cuttings of anything to do with addiction as I prepared
the manuscript. Many of the press quotations and illustrations in this book are the result of her thoughtful
background research. I do want to say thank you, therefore, to her.

Finally, I want to thank Alie, Philip, Hannah, and
Johnathan. I find it increasingly difficult to put into words
what I owe to them. The best thing is simply to say thank
you.

INTRODUCTION

In 1994 the following piece appeared in the national press, with the title 'Pizza de Résistance':

> For weeks, the world wondered if Bill Clinton could make up his mind, but as the Haiti showdown lurched towards a climax, the President finally reached a decision: he'd have a large veggie-pizza with extra broccoli.
>
> Four blocks away, at the K Street branch of Domino's Pizza, the chain's nearest outlet to the White House, manager Jim Czarnecki took personal command of operations. He didn't know much about foreign policy, but four years in Washington had taught Czarnecki the basics of crisis management.
>
> The world's leaders have their own ways of dealing with pressure: some turn to prayer, others to drink. Clinton orders pizza. 'You can pretty much tell the state of the nation by how many he eats', said Czarnecki.[1]

I include this piece at the beginning of this book for two reasons: first, because *O Brave New Church* is all about our popular mainstream culture, and everything about our culture – however trivial – has some significance as a sign of the times; and secondly, because it highlights a particular characteristic of our culture – the way in which we resort to mood-altering substances when the going gets tough. Indeed, my principal argument in this book is that ours is an addictive society in which the removal of pain is the highest priority. For President Clinton, it seems, eating pizza is the thing that helps to take the edge off reality. For others it may be sex or coffee or sport that, for a short time, alters moods and creates 'the feel-good factor'. Watching contemporary culture – particularly as it is communicated through the mass media – reveals that first-world societies like North America and Great Britain are fast becoming anaesthetised and numb through addict-ive behaviour.

Culture-watching is therefore a crucial ministry in the Church. This is really a 'watchman's' ministry, in the metaphorical sense used in the Book of Ezekiel. God told Ezekiel,

> 'Son of man, I have made you a watchman for the house of Israel.' (Ezek. 33:7)

Ezekiel's ministry, at least in part, involved watching the signs of the times. In ancient Israel, watchmen were posi-tioned on the highest points of the city walls in order to inform the people of approaching messengers or of pro-gress in battles outside. That is a graphic picture of what we need in the Church today. More than ever we need men and women on the battlements of the Church, observing the nature and the progress of culture, and, where necessary, highlighting the principalities and powers that need to be confronted. In a context like ours, in which our culture is falling into a collective numbness, watchmen are crucial to the mission of the Church and to the future health of society.

The gift of prophecy

I write as a charismatic Christian – that is to say, as a Christian who believes in the doctrine of 'baptism in the Holy Spirit', and in the use of the *charismata*, the spiritual gifts, today. Of particular importance to charismatic Christians (as to Pentecostals) is the spiritual gift of prophecy, by which is meant the supernatural ability to declare the mind of Christ in the form of a message, a pertinent passage of Scripture, a vision, a dream, a picture, or an impression. Charismatic Christians take seriously the fact that the events of Pentecost produced a democracy of the Spirit in which all people can now prophesy – including young people ('your sons and daughters', Acts 2:17), and old people too ('your old men will dream dreams'). As such, prophecy is actively taught, encouraged and practised in charismatic churches. In meetings of public worship, people are urged to proclaim the mind of Christ if the Holy Spirit so compels them. In many situations, this results in words being given to strengthen, encourage and comfort the Body of Christ (1 Cor. 14:3).

Saying this does not mean, however, that charismatics have got their theology and their praxis wholly right when it comes to the prophetic ministry itself. One of our most glaring weaknesses is the way we use this gift so individualistically. In practice this means a prophet sharing with another person – under the anointing of the Holy Spirit – things about that person's past, present or future. At best it may involve sharing the mind of Christ for a particular local church. But in my experience, that is usually as far as it goes. Rarely if ever do you hear people speaking out the kind of prophecy that we find on the lips of Ezekiel. Rarely do we hear people speaking an incisive word from the Lord about the culture in which we live. Wide-angled prophecy, in short, is noticeable by its absence.

What is urgently required, therefore, is a prophetic ministry of culture-watching. In other words, we need men and women called and equipped by the Spirit as watchmen. As Walter Brueggemann has written, prophecy in the Old Testament was much bigger than just a penetrating, supernatural word given to an individual or to a select group. It had much more to do with the creation of an alternative consciousness – an alternative to the false and idolatrous fields of perception in the world – and an alternative social reality. Thus, for Brueggemann,

> The task of prophetic ministry is to nurture, nourish, and evoke a consciousness and perception alternative to the consciousness and perception of the dominant culture around us. [Italics his][2]

The dominant culture

What is the dominant culture that the Church needs to scrutinise in its prophetic ministry right now? The dominant culture today is what Stan Wilson describes as 'popular culture': the culture

> of everyone in a society. It can be so pervasive that we seldom notice it. In order for us to notice it, we must step back and consciously observe it. We can do this by really looking around us at the objects in our society and asking ourselves why we idolize the things we do, why we buy the things we do, and why we believe in the things we do.[3]

Popular culture includes all the customs, beliefs, conventions and values that unconsciously affect our behaviour. Unlike high or élitist culture, in which these values are communicated to a minority through fine art, popular culture is disseminated to everyone through the mass media. This means that popular culture can only properly be understood if we take Stan Wilson's advice and stand back, consciously examining the pop music, the paperback novels, the adverts, the films, the soap operas, the computer technologies and the videos that both reflect and create contemporary culture. As we start to look more closely at such everyday signs, we become more and more aware of the cultural world around us. We become increasingly perceptive about the values that make us eat the things we eat, wear the things we wear, do the things we do. Examining the signs of the times makes us more conscious of popular culture, the culture that comprises all the customs, fads, symbols and activities that we generally take for granted.

The dominant culture is therefore popular culture. But can we be any more specific than this? Some try to use words like 'postmodern' to give a greater precision to the discussion. But the word 'postmodern' is really meaningless in its present form for a number of reasons: everyone disagrees about what it means; no one can decide whether 'modernism' has really finished yet; and often the best that can be said is that 'postmodernism' means 'that which comes after modernism'. This helps no one! Others use words like 'secularism' to describe the contemporary culture, with additional concepts like 'pluralism' and 'relativism' brought in to clarify what is meant. But here again there is tension. Many would argue that the main characteristic of secularism is the privatisation of religion – the compartmentalisation of religion into a private option rather than a public fact. Yet today the very opposite seems to be the case. Many religions (particularly of the New Age variety) are being marketed like consumer goods and quite openly, too. Indeed, today's religious consumer is free to 'pick'n'mix' in a very public way.

Neither postmodernism nor secularism seems to strike chords, especially with the average person in the street. A far more meaningful phrase is 'the addictive culture'. I will define addiction later on, but for now let us note that an addiction is a dependency upon any mood-altering substance, activity, belief, relationship or object. It is an anaesthetic to which we resort in order to mask the pains of life. It can be shopping, work, money, success, fitness, cleaning, perfectionism, fashion, cosmetics, food, chocolate, drugs – it can be just about anything. But the truth of the matter is that we are *all* doing something, everyday, to drive off the boredom, to mask the pain, and to take a holiday from reality. Some of us are more dependent on certain things than others. But we are all of us addicts, and we are all of us part of an addictive culture. Indeed, the advent of the National Lottery in Great Britain may well be the clearest proof of the evolution of an addictive culture – and indeed of the way in which the government of the day is actually colluding in making the culture addictive. A prophetic watching of the dominant culture is therefore a vital part of the Church's ministry. It is a ministry of protest in a time of spiritual and cultural oppression.

Walking the streets of Athens

The story of Paul's mission in Athens (Acts 17:22–34) provides a biblical paradigm for this observation of popular culture. Here Luke records that Paul spent several days touring Athens before he preached at the meeting of the Areopagus. He was, in effect, 'culture-watching'. Luke tells us that Paul 'walked around and looked carefully at the objects of worship in Athens'. Paul was, to use Stan Wilson's words, consciously observing the objects in that society and asking why the Athenians idolised the things they did. He was, in brief, analysing the culture. When he came to preach his message, he was able to use aspects of Athenian culture in order to make his message intelligible, relevant and incisive. Of particular significance is the fact that Paul quotes from the mainstream literature known by the Athenians. He comments, 'As some of your own poets have said, "We are God's offspring".' This quotation is from the poet Aratus (*c.*315–240 BC) and the poet Cleanthes (331–233 BC).

Paul's use of literature as a bridge between gospel and culture brings me to this present work, *O Brave New Church*, for my own book was born out of an experience of rereading a classic work of English literature: Aldous Huxley's futuristic novel, *Brave New World*, published in 1932. Reading that novel, and at the same time observing aspects of popular culture all around me, I suddenly became aware of the extraordinary relevance of Huxley's novel for today. I was forcibly struck by the way in which Huxley's story gives meaning to the story of our popular culture.

Take, for example, this description of Huxley's utopia:

> And she would tell him about the lovely music that came out of a box, and all the nice games you could play, and the delicious things to eat and drink, and the light that came when you pressed a little thing in the wall, and the pictures that you could hear and feel and smell, as well as see, and another box for making nice smells, and the pink and green and blue

> and silver houses as high as mountains . . . and the
> boxes where you could see and hear what was hap-
> pening at the other side of the world . . .[4]

In this extract Huxley, with uncanny vision, foresees a
society of home cinema and video software, of hi-fi and
personal stereos, of computing and multi-media, of television and telecommunications, of Sega and Nintendo, of
modems and home technology – everything, in fact, that
you can now see each year at consumer electronics shows.
Huxley, in short, predicted with startling accuracy the
kind of culture that is emerging in the nineties. That
culture – which is popular or mainstream culture – is one
that is high on what Huxley himself called 'technological
narcotics'. In fact, it is a society high on all kinds of
anaesthetic agents, from shopping to Disneyland, from
virtual reality to drugs such as ecstasy. Huxley foresaw a
society just like ours, in which everyone had willingly
succumbed to an oppression not of pain but of pleasure.
Indeed, had Paul walked our streets in Britain today, I like
to think that he would have quoted not from Cleanthes or
Aratus but from the writings of Aldous Huxley – in
particular, from the haunting novel *Brave New World*.

Cultivating an alternative consciousness

Most of us are not aware of popular culture at all because
we take it for granted, like the air we breathe. Christian
apologists who write on this subject reveal an awareness
of some intellectual trends in society, such as secularism,
pluralism and relativism (often analysed under the rubric
of 'postmodernism'). However, even these writers reveal a
neglect of what is really going on in mainstream, everyday

culture. In my own attempt at culture-watching I have spent a good deal of time not merely studying Huxley's works but also watching films, attending exhibitions, reading magazines, looking at newspapers, recording and studying advertisements, looking through video shops, playing computer games, listening to compact discs, visiting Alton Towers, and so on. Much of my book is therefore a diagnosis of popular culture using aspects of high culture as well as folk culture. I justify the use of both on the grounds that the sharp dividing line between élite and popular culture has all but disappeared today. Indeed, this collapse of 'high' versus 'folk' culture is a major characteristic of our times – why else are films and detective fiction studied in universities?

The argument of this short book is simple. In Chapter 1 I will provide a brief summary of Huxley's *Brave New World*, and make some comments concerning its overall relevance for understanding popular culture. In Chapter 2 I will look at some more precise parallels between Huxley's utopia and contemporary, mainstream culture. In Chapter 3 I will examine one particular parallel, eroticism. In Chapter 4 I will move from observation to evaluation: using Anne Wilson Schaef's seminal work, *When Society Becomes an Addict*, I will explain why our present culture has centred itself on one particular value, the removal of pain. Finally, in Chapter 5, I will describe some of the areas upon which Christians in Britain need to focus if we are to become a 'brave new Church' – in other words, a radical community of resistance and liberation which will help to shape a better world in a time of cultural transition. In the Conclusion, we will return once again to Aldous Huxley.

My main prayer, in this highly addictive culture, is that God himself will take hold of us and show us the far

more liberating, more euphoric, more wholesome way of
the Spirit-filled life. My prayer is, in conclusion, the
prayer of St Augustine:

'Oh, that thou wouldst inebriate my soul!'

1 'O BRAVE NEW WORLD!'

'O brave new world,' he began, then suddenly
interrupted himself; the blood had left his
cheeks; he was as pale as paper.[1]

On 26 July 1894, a century ago, one of the outstanding
writers of the twentieth century was born. His name was
Aldous Huxley, and his most famous work was to be the
futuristic novel *Brave New World*, published in 1932. Other
books were to achieve notoriety – such as *Eyeless in Gaza*,
Crome Yellow, *Antic Hay*, *The Doors of Perception* and *Jesting
Pilate* – but *Brave New World* would tower above them all
in terms of its prophetic insights. Somehow Huxley foresaw, with amazing accuracy, the kind of society that is
now being formed all around us. He cleverly anticipated
that the results of trends which he perceived in his own
day would produce a society, like ours, that was pro-
foundly hedonistic in character. Today, at the edge of the
third millenium, Huxley's science fiction seems alarmingly
close to actual fact.

Huxley's centenary

Aldous Huxley is again in the public eye. 1994 was the
centenary of his birth, and Flamingo publishers republished all of his books.

Huxley has now surpassed George Orwell in terms of

popularity. Orwell wrote several futuristic novels, notably *Nineteen Eighty-Four* and *Animal Farm*. Published in 1949, his novel *Nineteen Eighty-Four* anticipated a thoroughly oppressive, communist society in which Big Brother was always watching you. This so disturbed people that when the actual year arrived, the Western world held its breath. Would Orwell's predictions come true? In the end 1984 came and went with no noticeable disturbances. As Neil Postman observed,

> The roots of liberal democracy had held. Wherever else the terror has happened, we, at least, had not been visited by Orwellian nightmares.[2]

As 1985 began, widespread relief was followed by a new complacency. People recognized that Western democracies were not about to be transformed into communist regimes. So capitalism reasserted itself and, in the process, we forgot something very important: that

> alongside Orwell's dark vision, there was another – slightly older, slightly less well known, equally chilling: Aldous Huxley's *Brave New World*.[3]

The differences between *Nineteen Eighty-Four* and *Brave New World* could not be more stark. Both depict forms of social oppression, but the nature and the means of that oppression are markedly different. Postman puts it thus:

> Contrary to common belief even among the educated, Huxley and Orwell did not prophesy the same thing. Orwell warns that we will be overcome by an externally imposed oppression. But in Huxley's vision, no Big Brother is required to deprive people of their autonomy, maturity and history. As he saw it, people will come to love their oppression, to

adore the technologies which undo their capacities to think.[4]

Postman's view, expressed in his book *Amusing Ourselves to Death*, is that the society that Huxley predicted is the one that is most likely to emerge in the liberal democracies of the Western world – in other words, a society in which the oppression would be one of pleasure rather than pain. I believe he is right. In the next few pages I will therefore provide a brief summary of Huxley's future society, before returning at the end of the chapter to this notion of oppression. In all of this, I want to make the point that 1994 was of far greater significance than 1984: in years to come, the centenary of Huxley's birth will be regarded as more significant than the date of Orwell's imagined new world order.

A new world order

Brave New World begins with a terse and dramatic description:

> A squat grey building of only thirty-four storeys. Over the main entrance the words, CENTRAL LONDON HATCHERY AND CONDITIONING CENTRE, and, in a shield, the World State's motto, COMMUNITY, IDENTITY, STABILITY.[5]

In this building human eggs are fertilised through a laboratory process monitored by the Director of Hatcheries and Conditioning. They are then kept alive and actively developed in incubators. Each egg is assigned a predetermined social status and role. There are five classes – Alphas, Betas, Gammas, Deltas and Epsilons.

Once the babies are born, they are subject to 'neo-Pavlovian conditioning'. Genetic engineering is fine for keeping a society populated, but social conditioning must be added to this process if the society is to remain stable. So once the babies become children, they are subject to brainwashing. This is achieved through communal education (including electric shock treatment) and hypnopaedia ('sleep teaching'). Before a child awakes in the morning, he or she has the following kinds of information played from a recorder beneath the pillow:

> 'Alpha children wear grey. They work much harder than we do, because they're so frightfully clever. I'm really awfully glad I'm a Beta, because I don't work so hard. And then we are much better than the Gammas and Deltas. Gammas are stupid. They all wear green, and Delta children wear khaki. Oh no, I *don't* want to play with Delta children. And Epsilons are still worse . . .'[6]

A world of technological narcotics

It is one thing to create and to condition people like this, but it is quite another for them to tolerate and even enjoy such an existence. So whilst the Director of Hatcheries works hard to create and condition, ten figures known as the World Controllers work equally hard to produce a society in which there is 'no leisure from pleasure'. These World Controllers maintain stability by keeping the citizens as numb as possible through the effective use of pleasure. The World Controller who features prominently in *Brave New World* is Mustapha Mond, and he is in no doubt about how to keep people happy:

> Seven and a half hours of mild, unexhausting labour, and then the *soma* ration and games and unrestricted copulation and the feelies. What more can they ask for?[7]

In this kind of hedonistic society, people learn from the earliest age to like their 'unescapable social destiny'. Right from the start, people are given a limitless means of taking holidays from reality. In Mustapha Mond's words just quoted, a number of these mood-altering substances and processes are identified. The *soma* ration is a hallucinogenic drug which helps people to take a trip out of the mundane world of work they have just left. The games vary, but sophisticated, technological sports like 'electromagnetic golf' prove to be very popular. 'Unrestricted copulation' is another avenue of pleasure. In a society where everyone is 'decanted', everyone belongs to everyone else: sex is therefore a lawful means of escapism. So are the 'feelies', a form of cinema in which you can actually 'feel' what is happening on the screen.

All these, and many more, are used to create a corporate numbness. With everyone taking regular holidays from reality, who needs to take up arms against the system? Whilst there is 'no leisure from pleasure', people have no awareness of their slavery. As Mustapha Mond puts it,

> 'Now – such is progress – the old men work, the old men copulate, the old men have no time, no leisure from pleasure, not a moment to sit down and think – or if ever by some unlucky chance such a crevice of time should yawn in the solid substance of their distractions, there is always *soma*, delicious

soma, half a gramme for a half-holiday, a gramme
for a week-end, two grammes for a trip to the
gorgeous East, three for a dark eternity on the moon;
returning whence they find themselves on the other
side of the crevice, safe on the solid ground of
daily labour and distraction, scampering from feely
to feely, from girl to pneumatic girl, from Electromagnetic Golf Course to . . .'[8]

The runaway world

The world that Huxley describes is therefore one in which
a highly advanced technology of escapism has evolved.
Here is a society in which there seems to be no pain. It
is a society in which reality is not allowed to surface for
a moment. It is truly a hedonistic, runaway world.

What, then, are the realities that the World Controllers
are most eager for their wards to avoid? There are essen-
tially three: 'Time and Death and God'.

First of all, Time. In *Brave New World*, years are counted
from the introduction of the Ford Model-T motor car.
The year the novel begins is A.F. (after Ford) 632. Everything prior to Henry Ford's invention is obliterated from
memory. It is not taught, and any attempt to investigate it
is ruthlessly quashed. There is, in fact, an active campaign
against the past. Museums were closed long ago. Historical
monuments were blown up. All books published before A.F.
150 were suppressed. The whole of society is constructed
in such a way as to prevent an awareness of time. The
important thing is to live in the fullness of the present
moment. There is total amnesia about the past (life before
Ford). There is total anaesthesia about the future (especially
death). People are numb to everything except the passing

moment – and even that can be blotted out by a ration of *soma*.

The result is that the reality of Death, secondly, is pushed to one side. I have made the point already that Huxley's dystopia employs every conceivable means to remove the pain of life. There are only a few remaining diseases which can be caught. If you are unlucky enough to contract a fatal one, there is always the Park Lane Hospital for the Dying. Here the atmosphere is kept continuously alive with happy melodies. At the foot of every bed there is a TV which is left on, like a running tap, from morning till night. Every quarter of an hour the prevailing perfume of the room is automatically changed. Cups of caffeine solution are served and chocolate éclairs are constantly on offer. As one nurse puts it,

> 'We try . . . to create a thoroughly pleasant atmos-
> phere here – something between a first-class hotel
> and a feely-palace . . .'9

If Time and Death are realities to be forgotten, so thirdly is God. There is a lot of talk about God in *Brave New World*. Even though godliness has been replaced by fordliness, God is still discussed, but only in the highest circles. Mustapha Mond's views are particularly interesting. He regards works like the Bible, *The Imitation of Christ* and *The Varieties of Religious Experience* as 'porno-graphic old books'. They are quite simply taboo. Why? Because such books teach that we are not masters of our own destiny but people made in the image of God, made to serve the purposes of God. They teach that we are God's property, not our own; and that our happiness lies in serving God, not in serving ourselves.

The reason why these books are banned as 'smut' is obvious: such truths are in direct conflict with the values

of Our Ford and the World Controllers. Mustapha Mond
and the rest teach that 'we can be independent of God'.
They teach that the losses for which religion compensates
can be compensated by other means (*soma* and the rest).
They teach that 'God isn't compatible with machinery and
scientific medicine and universal happiness'. Start talking
about God and you are compelled to start talking about
'self-denial'. This cannot be allowed to happen: social
stability depends upon hedonism, not asceticism.

The problem of pain

However, the problem of pain is not eradicated with 100
per cent efficacy in *Brave New World*. The central character
of the novel is an Alpha-Plus intellectual called Bernard
Marx. He is a man who cannot get rid of the sense of
'shame' in his life. By 'shame' I mean the feeling that he
is a misfit, a failure, a mistake. The reason for this lies
principally in his physical appearance. His society is conditioned to believe that men should be tall and well built.
'Indeed, a faint hypnopaedic prejudice in favour of size
was universal.' Unfortunately, Bernard is short and thin,
and the common gossip is that something went wrong in
the Centre for Hatcheries and Conditioning – that too
much alcohol solution was put in his blood-surrogate.
The men whom he meets are therefore prone to play
practical jokes on him. The women laugh at him. This
only compounds the problem:

> The mockery made him feel an outsider; and feeling
> an outsider he behaved like one, which increased
> the prejudice against him and intensified the con-
> tempt and hostility aroused by his physical defects.

Which in turn increased his sense of being alien and alone.[10]

Bernard is therefore an outsider. He begins to yearn for danger, not comfort; for freedom, not slavery; for real feelings, not superficial stimulation. Indeed, whenever he is introduced, words like 'melancholy' and 'pain' abound. His pain is intensified towards the beginning of the novel when he falls in love with the beautiful, 'wonderfully pneumatic' Lenina Crowne, an uncommonly pretty nurse who works in the Embryo Store. Emotionally she is the exact opposite of Bernard. She is a conformer, trotting out all the platitudes of her conditioning: for example, 'never put off till to-morrow the fun you can have to-day'. Her feeling about Bernard is that he is 'Odd, odd, odd'.

However, these two people become lovers when Bernard manages to acquire a permit to visit the New Mexican Reservation. He invites Lenina to accompany him and she accepts. Few people are allowed to go there because this is where the 'savages' live. Lenina regards the opportunity as too good to miss, and so they arrive by ship at the pueblo of Malpais. They are taken by their Indian guide to the reservation where the smell, the dirt, the rubbish and the poverty are immediately oppressive. Lenina is disgusted; 'cleanliness is next to fordliness', she says. She fumbles in her pocket for her supply of *soma*, but finds that she has left the bottle behind at the rest-house. She is therefore 'left to face the horrors of Malpais unaided'.

As they go deeper into the heart of the reservation, they start to hear drums. Hideously masked dancers start to appear from underground chambers and start dancing in a circle, constantly chanting as the speed of the rhythm increases. The chief dancer takes black snakes from a chest and throws them amongst the dancers. Then the music dies down. A young boy emerges, and as he dances round the snakes he is whipped. The blood runs from his wounds but he keeps dancing. Eventually he collapses, face down in the dust amidst the snakes. The dancing ends. The drums stop beating. The boy's body is removed, and all is quiet. Lenina, shocked by the sight of pain (something from which she has been shielded for so long), can only say, 'Oh, I wish I had my *soma*.'

The noble savage

At this point, Huxley introduces another key character. His name is John. He speaks flawless English and is quite unlike the Indian natives in the pueblo. Later we will learn that he is the son of the Director of Hatcheries and Conditioning, and that he and his mother Linda were exiled to the reservation many years before. John tells Lenina and Bernard that he wishes he had been the sacrificial victim in the dance they have just witnessed. 'They could have had twice as much blood from me', he says. Lenina is intrigued. 'Do you mean to say that you *wanted* to be hit with that whip?' she asks. Yes, says John: 'to show that I can bear pain without crying out.'

Bernard becomes fascinated with John and manages to take him back to 'civilisation'. There John is known as 'the Savage' and becomes a celebrity misfit. John, after all, has a totally different world-view. For him, the cure for unhappiness lies in embracing suffering, not in indulging in pleasure. He confides in Bernard that he once stood against a rock in the middle of the day, in summer, with his arms stretched out like Jesus on the cross. When

Bernard asks why, John replies that he wanted to know what it was like being crucified, hanging there in the heat of the sun. Bernard feels a degree of empathy with that.

As Bernard starts to show John off to his peers, he finds that his own sense of alienation disappears. He becomes a celebrity.

> The days passed. Success went fizzily to Bernard's head, and in the process completely reconciled him (as any good intoxicant should do) to a world which, up till then, he had found very unsatisfactory.[11]

Linda, John's mother, meanwhile, finds the shock of her experiences all too much. For Linda, the return to civilisation is only managed by asking for more and more rations of *soma*:

> The holiday it gave was perfect and, if the morning after was disagreeable, it was so, not intrinsically, but only by comparison with the joys of the holiday. The remedy was to make the holiday continuous. Greedily she clamoured for ever larger, ever more frequent doses. Dr Shaw at first demurred; then let her have what she wanted. She took as much as twenty grammes a day.[12]

So whilst Bernard becomes more and more intoxicated by success, Linda becomes more and more intoxicated by *soma*. The Savage, however, grows more and more unhappy. He cannot abide the attractions of this so-called civilised society. He finds the feelies an ignoble experience. He regards *soma* as a poison to soul as well as body. The 'brave new world' starts to lose its alluring lustre. When the Savage starts to act on this revulsion, Mustapha Mond steps in and he is arrested. John spends the rest of his days in a self-chosen hermitage, an old lighthouse

which stands on the crest of a hill between Puttenham
and Elstead. He throws himself into a lifestyle of ascetism,
trying by all means to rid himself of the pollution of this
brave new world:

> From time to time he stretched out his arms as
> though he were on the cross, and held them thus
> through long minutes of an ache that gradually
> increased till it became a tremulous and excruciating
> agony; held them, in voluntary crucifixion, while
> he repeated, through clenched teeth (the sweat,
> meanwhile, pouring down his face), 'Oh, forgive
> me! Oh, make me pure! Oh, help me to be good!'
> again and again, till he was on the point of fainting
> from the pain.[13]

From here on, the downfall of the Savage is inexorable.

At the edge of the nightmare

Having had a glimpse of Brave New World, it is hard not
to spot some of the parallels with contemporary society.
Huxley himself wrote, fifteen years after the publication
of Brave New World, that most of the ingredients of his
'happier and more stable world' were probably no more
than three or four generations away. He anticipated that
society would develop more sophisticated means of
suggestion, better substitutes for alcohol and narcotics,
and a foolproof system of eugenics. Even in 1946 he saw
evidence in the USA of the sexual promiscuity of Brave
New World. He wrote:

> There are already certain American cities in which
> the number of divorces is equal to the number of

marriages. In a few years, no doubt, marriage licences will be sold like dog licences, good for a period of twelve months, with no law against changing dogs or keeping more than one animal at a time.[14]

Little wonder that he was to add,

Today it seems quite possible that the horror may be upon us within a single century. That is, if we refrain from blowing ourselves to smithereens in the interval.[15]

In 1959, four years before his death, Huxley published *Brave New World Revisited*, a collection of non-fictional essays in which he compared facets of his futuristic society with trends in the West just before the 1960s. This collection begins with the sentence,

In 1931, when *Brave New World* was being written, I was convinced that there was still plenty of time.[16]

However, by 1959 Huxley was more pessimistic:

Twenty-seven years later, in this third quarter of the twentieth century AD., and long before the end of the first century AF., I feel a good deal less optimistic than I did when I was writing *Brave New World*. The prophecies made in 1931 are coming true much sooner than I thought they would.[17]

By the time Huxley died in 1963 (on the same day that President John F. Kennedy was assassinated), the nightmare was about to become a reality.

The neglect of *Brave New World*

If *Brave New World* is so prophetic, we might justly ask
why it has, until very recently, been so neglected. I gave
an answer to that question at the beginning of this chapter,
and it is to this thought that we now return. The neglect
of *Brave New World* has been mainly due to the popularity of Orwell's *Nineteen Eighty-Four*. Until the collapse
of Communism in the former Soviet Union, many people
in the Western world had a deep-seated fear that Orwell's
vision would some day become a reality. However, with
the destruction of the Berlin Wall, the threat of Communism all but disappeared and the disturbing spectre of
totalitarianism was apparently exorcised. All seemed to be
well in the world.

It was precisely at this point that we ought to have
turned from Orwell to Huxley, for Huxley rightly saw
that there are in fact two different kinds of totalitarianism.
Writing in 1946, Huxley wrote this about what he called
'the old kind' of totalitarianism:

> Government by clubs and firing squads, by artificial
> famine, mass imprisonment, and mass deportation,
> is not merely inhumane . . .; it is demonstrably
> inefficient.[18]

This kind of totalitarianism, Huxley argued, would not
endure. However, there is, he proposed, a 'new' kind of
totalitarianism which will prove to be far more durable.
Of this new kind, Huxley had this to say:

> A really efficient totalitarian state would be one in
> which the all-powerful executive of political bosses
> and their army of managers control a population of

slaves who do not have to be coerced, because they
love their servitude.[19]

It is this kind of society that Huxley describes in *Brave
New World*, and which he saw emerging in the world
around him. Today it seems even more likely that Huxley
was right and Orwell wrong, for capitalism has proved to
be far more resilient than Communism. Perhaps the most
memorable indication of this was on 31 January 1990,
when TV news reports showed 30,000 Russians queueing
up for nearly two hours outside the golden arches of the
first McDonald's restaurant in Moscow. At the time, this
was the largest McDonald's in the world, with 700 seats
and 650 employees. From that day on, the queue at
lunchtime contained, on average, 1200 people, each
taking 90 minutes to reach the counter.

Why is the arrival of McDonald's in Moscow so
important? Perhaps because after years of communist
oppression and austerity, Moscovites were at last being
allowed a taste of capitalist freedom and prosperity. After
years of drab ennui, Russians were entering the golden
arches to a world of milk shakes, cola, burgers, chips,
glitzy surroundings, colourful packaging, momentary
community and, of course, 'pleasure'. If that is so, then
in future years, the construction of the McDonald's restaurant in Moscow may well be regarded as an event of
epochal significance – as epochal as the destruction of the
Berlin Wall. It may well come to symbolise the exchange
of one form of oppression for another – the old kind of
totalitarianism for the new.

The neglect of *Brave New World* therefore has a lot to
do with the Western paranoia about communist totalitarianism and the fear that Orwell's dream would come
true. But Huxley himself warned us, in *Brave New World*

Revisited, that his own vision was more probable than Orwell's. Huxley summed up the differences between *Nineteen Eighty-Four* and *Brave New World* as follows:

> In *Nineteen Eighty-Four* the lust for power is satisfied by inflicting pain; in *Brave New World*, by inflicting a hardly less humiliating pleasure.[20]

Huxley had seen that in an age of advanced technology, oppression would more probably come from a system with a smiling face than from one whose countenance elicits hatred.[21] He had seen that England was much more likely to produce a right-wing totalitarianism of pleasure and denial, than a left-wing totalitarianism of pain and suppression. It is this form of oppression that the Church of the nineties needs to confront.

2 OUR SOCIAL DESTINY

'Try to imagine what "living with one's family"
meant.'
    They tried; but obviously without the small-
est success.[1]

The *Demolition Man*

Obviously, *Brave New World* depicts a hedonistic society in
the extremist possible way. But Huxley's use of hyperbole
should not be allowed to become a distraction in itself.
The fact is that the trends which Huxley saw in the 1930s
are now so obvious that a society not unlike that of *Brave
New World* is becoming more and more likely. Indeed,
hardly a month seems to go by without some sector of
popular culture drawing parallels with Huxley's dystopia.
    Take, for example, Marco Brambilla's 1993 film, *Demo-
lition Man*, starring Sylvester Stallone. This portrays the
society of Los Angeles (now called San Angeles) in
the year 2032. The main character, called John Spartan
(after the savage called 'John' in Huxley's novel), is frozen
in 1996 for an unintentional manslaughter of thirty hos-
tages who were taken by an arch-criminal called Simon
Phoenix. Phoenix is also put into deep-freeze in the
same high-tech penitentiary. Whilst frozen, a process of
hypnopaedic rehabilitation takes place. Simon Phoenix
is released in 2036, supposedly cured of his homicidal
tendencies.

The society into which Phoenix is released is a police
state run on the lines of *Brave New World*. It is a society
with self-esteem booths, where people can be cheered up
through affirming messages about their beauty and worth.
It is a society with no swearing, no stealing, in fact no
crime at all. It is a place with endless distractions for
pleasure.

Unfortunately, Phoenix has not been successfully
rehabilitated and starts running amok, murdering all who
stand in his path. John, a highly unorthodox and aggressive
police sergeant, is then prematurely unfrozen in order to
apprehend Phoenix. John collaborates with Lenina
Huxley (another reference to *Brave New World*), who takes
quite a liking to him. At one point she invites him to
have sex with her. He accepts the offer and prepares
himself. Lenina comes into his flat with two virtual-reality
headsets and a couple of flannels. What John has not had
time to appreciate is that all sexual intercourse is con-
ducted through the medium of interactive video. There
is no exchange of body fluids. Sex happens in the hygienic
world of computer-generated graphics.

Not surprisingly, the influence of John and Phoenix in
this 'brave new world' (a phrase actually used by the police
chief) is devastating. The whole nature of the society
changes dramatically. Towards the end of the movie,
Phoenix is horribly killed and John actually manages to
kiss Lenina. They walk off, hand in hand, into a much
braver world – supposedly – than the one he entered.
This is a world where people can now learn to feel again.
In the final analysis, therefore, it was the people of San
Angeles who really needed thawing out, not John Spartan.

The new childbirth technologies

Stories like these reveal the current indebtedness to
Huxley in popular culture. If you look hard enough,
you will find echoes of Huxley's hedonistic dystopia in
everything from the science fiction of Bill Gibson to
television series like *Wild Palms* (Oliver Stone). However,
such Huxleyan narratives usually have two things in
common – they are futuristic and they are fictional. What
of the society in which we live right now? What of
contemporary British culture? Are there any signs of a
Brave New Worldian order already emerging in everyday
reality?

Let us recall for a moment that the society of *Brave
New World* is one in which human beings are genetically
engineered. Humans are born through a well-orchestrated
process of eugenics. Is such a process scientifically feasible
in contemporary society? Has science advanced suf-
ficiently to enable us to use genetic engineering for purposes of social determinism?

In a leader article for the *Daily Telegraph* dated 16
August 1993, and headed 'Brave new world', the public
was warned of new advances in genetics. Apparently it
will soon be possible to 'improve' the human breeding
stock by genetic engineering. It will be possible not only
to eliminate hereditary diseases but also to cultivate intelli-
gence, beauty and skill. As this expertise develops, some
scientists have become worried that genetics may be
moving too fast for thorough moral reflection. On 15
August 1993, therefore, an international conference of
genetics was held in Birmingham, and one of its aims was
to ask questions about ethical responsibility. As the leader
writer put it:

The fear of responsible scientists is that an irrespon-
sible section of their brethren will align themselves
with an ill thought out degree of public enthusiasm,
and go rushing off in search of perfect babies, alter-
ing or discarding those deemed imperfect in order
to achieve a strictly utilitarian brave new world.[2]

Obviously these advances in genetics need to be very
carefully monitored. Breakthroughs in genetics should not
be used to establish a society of ideal human beings.
Those politicians who tend to see the most important
determinant of society as genetic rather than environmental need to be very closely watched and advised in this
regard. There is already evidence of some societies moving
in this direction in order to eliminate certain categories
of people. In China, a new law on eugenics and health
protection has been passed making it illegal for people
suffering from sexually transmitted diseases, mental ill-
nesses or hepatitis to marry. The law also assures abortions
and sterilisations to avoid new births of inferior quality
and to heighten the standards of the whole population.

Such trends are worrying – so worrying in fact that on
2 January 1994 Neville Hodgkinson asked,

Despite the good intentions of our doctors and legis-
lators, might the day not yet come when human
beings, graded according to genetically determined
functions, are hatched Brave New World-style from
incubators, and brought up in communal nurseries?[3]

As Hodgkinson concluded, 'the technology is there'.

So the new childbirth technologies suggest that Huxley's dream *could* come true. Maybe in the future we will
see more front-page headlines like this one published on
9 February 1992:

COUPLE GIVE AWAY FROZEN BABY

A British couple are to become the first to give away their unborn babies, now stored on ice in a London clinic.

Embryos saved and frozen after Alice and Leslie Turner successfully underwent treatment for infertility are to be offered to another couple as part of a Brave New World 'adoption before birth' scheme.[4]

Perhaps we are not all that far from an age of 'designer babies'.

The extinction of the family

In *Brave New World*, babies are delivered in the Centre for Hatcheries; they are not born into families. There are no families in Huxley's dystopia because there are no fathers or mothers. Everyone is fertilised and 'decanted' in Centres for Hatcheries and Conditioning. Indeed, words like 'father', 'mother', 'birth' and 'home' are all regarded as smut. This is a society in which people can no longer imagine what it is like to have a 'viviparous' mother (that is, a mother who gives birth to and rears her own young). When the Director of Hatcheries and Conditioning takes his students round the centre for a guided tour, he talks about the distant past when people had 'mothers'. There is an embarrassing silence which is only broken by the Director's words,

'These', he said gravely, 'are unpleasant facts; I know it. But, then, most historical facts *are* unpleasant.'[5]

The point hardly needs making that there are disturbing signs of the future extinction of the traditional, functional

family in contemporary society. A perceptive observer of
these trends in British society is the American writer
Charles Murray. He has recently demonstrated that there
has been an alarming growth in illegitimacy in Britain,
the like of which has never been witnessed in our history.
The following graph makes this plain (the statistics are
taken from parish ecclesiastical records until the 1840s,
and from the civil register thereafter):[6]

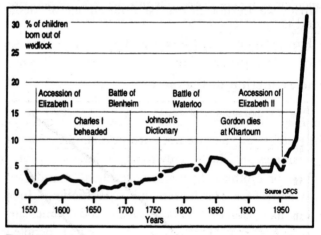

The History

These figures are disquieting. In 1987, when Charles
Murray first wrote on this subject, 23 per cent of English
births were outside marriage; by 1992 this had jumped
to 31 per cent. As Murray puts it, 'Britain has *never* seen
anything like what has happened in the last 15 years.'
'Almost one in every three children is currently being
born outside marriage.'[7]

Murray goes on to point out that these statistics point
to the breakdown of the British family, but that this
breakdown is occurring in drastically different ways in
different parts of society. Put very simply, he claims that

a new class is emerging which he calls 'the New Victorians'. This comprises the dominant economic class of professionals and executives who are resisting the trends of modernity and returning to the traditional values of monogamous marriage with children. At the same time, another class is emerging which he describes as 'the New Rabble'. This is a class in which the family has effectively collapsed. It is mainly but not exclusively focused in the inner cities where crime, illegitimacy and single parenthood (Murray contends) are rife.

From this analysis, Murray proposes one of two scenarios for the Britain of the future. Scenario 1 is what he

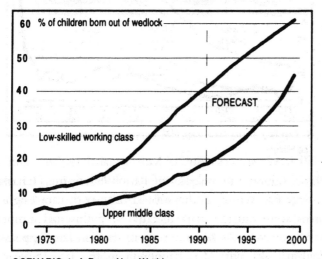

SCENARIO 1: A Brave New World

calls 'the Brave New World' scenario. In this forecast, both the affluent and educated sections of society (what he calls 'the upper middle class') and 'the low-skilled working class' continue to witness a collapse of traditional family values and a rise in illegitimacy.[8]

Scenario 2 is what Murray calls 'the New Victorians and the New Rabble'. In this forecast, the low-skilled working class experiences increasing illegitimacy and family breakdown, whilst the upper middle class reacts against these trends with a new puritanism. As this happens, society starts to polarise into an 'overclass' and an 'underclass':[9]

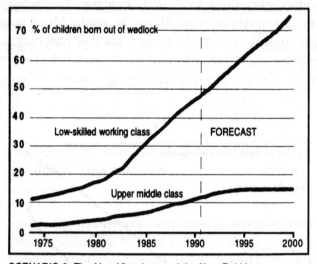

SCENARIO 2: The New Victorians and the New Rabble

Whatever our criticisms of Murray's analysis, one cannot deny the *general* plausibility of his observations. The rise in illegitimacy is an undeniable statistic with catastrophic consequences. In this respect, Huxley's picture of a society of designer babies may not be as remote as it at first appears. The alarm bells should be ringing now.

The power of advertising

Another worrying parallel between contemporary society and Huxley's dystopia lies in the phenomenon of social conditioning. In *Brave New World*, human beings are not only conceived through 'eugenics' (a word meaning 'well born' or 'of good birth'), they are also conditioned through a long process of hypnopaedia ('sleep teaching'). The most common form of this is recordings of various value statements which are broadcast through the pillows of children as they sleep. These value statements are called 'hypnopaedic proverbs'. One example is 'Everyone belongs to everyone else.' When Mustapha Mond meets some students outside the Central London Hatchery and Conditioning Centre, he utters this 'hypnopaedic proverb' and the narrator describes the response of the audience:

> The students nodded, emphatically agreeing with a statement which upwards of sixty-two thousand repetitions in the dark had made them accept, not merely as true, but as axiomatic, self-evident, utterly indisputable.[10]

It might seem on the surface that contemporary society has no real parallel for this kind of subliminal education. But when Huxley wrote *Brave New World Revisited* in 1959, he pointed to one particular phenomenon in mass culture which he regarded as very similar: the power of advertising. In his chapter on 'The arts of selling', Huxley wrote a quite brilliant critique of the sales strategy of the average advertiser. This was his satirical advice to any aspiring advertising manager:

> Find some common desire, some widespread uncon-scious fear or anxiety; think about some way to relate this wish or fear to the product you have to sell; then build a bridge of verbal or pictorial symbols over which your customer can pass from fact to compensatory dream, and from the dream to the

illusion that your product, when purchased, will make your dream come true.[11]

Huxley argued that the success of this kind of salesmanship depends upon its power over the subconscious mind. Countless symbols and images are transmitted from magazine, TV and cinema adverts into the subconscious. More powerful still, innumerable proverbs are welcomed into the unconscious through visual and auditory media. Statements like 'We know the meaning of cleaning' take the place that was once occupied by proverbs from the world of literature, Scripture and nursery rhymes. As Huxley observed:

> In my childhood we were taught to sing nursery rhymes and, in pious households, hymns. Today the little ones warble the Singing Commercials. Which is better – 'Rheingold is my beer, the dry beer', or 'Hey diddle-diddle, the cat and the fiddle'? 'Abide with me' or 'You'll wonder where the yellow went, when you brush your teeth with Pepsodent?' Who knows?[12]

Today, many would claim that advertising provides the 'hypnopaedic proverbs' that we hear on everyone's lips in *Brave New World*. The images that are used to sell products are ones that resonate with our deepest desires and needs; they are images connoting youth, beauty, fashion, happiness, sexuality, success, serenity, luxury and status. The average American adult is exposed to about five hundred such images *every day*. Indeed, by the time he or she has reached the age of 21, it is estimated that this person will have been exposed to between one and two million advertisements.[13] In contemporary society, therefore, we are born into a lifelong exposure to images which both reflect and alter our lifestyles.

Some argue that such adverts have a minimal effect on the majority of people. However, in the 1950s Vance Packard produced a book called *Hidden Persuaders* in which he showed how advertisers were employing the techniques of motivational research (MR) in order to sell their goods. He accused advertisers of using 'depth manipulation'. More recently this research has been updated. In the 1970s Wilson Key contended that advertisers were using sexually explicit hidden messages, called 'subliminal imbeds', to sell products. This research was written up in three popular books during the 1980s: *Subliminal Seduction*, *Media Sexploitation*, and *Clam Plate Orgy*. Key was convinced that adverts were designed in order to appeal to our instincts about death, sex and fear.

Academics have not yet decided whether advertisements really do have a subliminal power over people, or indeed whether advertisers are consciously employing subliminal persuaders in the selling of their products. However, whilst it is possible to go too far in criticising the advertising industry, it would be naive too to assume that those who construct modern adverts are ignorant about hidden persuaders. At the end of the 1980s, Schweppes produced a ninety-second commercial featuring a man expressing concern over subliminal advertising. During the course of the commercial, the word 'Schweppes' flashed continuously on the screen. A recent advert for Absolut Vodka also made reference to this phenomenon in a magazine advert which portrayed a glass of vodka silhouetted against a dark background, with the words ABSOLUT SUBLIMINAL as its headline. Stan Wilson also records the following incident:

During the summer of 1990, Pepsi-Cola was criti-
cized by some consumers who claimed that the word
sex seemed to be subtly printed on the exterior of
a newly released Pepsi 'Cool Can'. A Pepsi spokes-
man said that it was merely an 'odd coincidence' and
that the design was selected only because consumers
preferred it over hundreds of other designs.[14]

Although it is very hard to prove conclusively, there
does seem to be some evidence that modern advertisements are created in order to trigger subconscious
emotional responses. The subliminal imbedding theory
would further suggest that this is an intentional strategy
on the part of some elements of the advertising industry,
and that some contemporary adverts may very well provide an analogy for Huxley's 'hypnopaedic proverbs'.
Again, *Brave New World* seems disturbingly relevant.

The evolution of the VALS matrix

If there are parallels between Huxley's eugenics and contemporary genetics, and between Huxley's hypnopaedia
and contemporary advertising, there are also parallels
between Huxley's stratification of society and contemporary trends. Readers of *Brave New World* will recall that
people are allocated a particular class whilst they are being
developed in the Centre for Hatcheries and Conditioning.
There are basically five classes or predetermined castes:
Alphas, Betas, Gammas, Deltas and Epsilons. Alphas are
intellectuals, Epsilons are workers. Social stability depends
upon the differences between these classes being main-
tained and reinforced. Consequently, 'elementary class
consciousness' is taught to children from the word go.

Now obviously there are no exact parallels with such social predeterminism in contemporary society. John Major, as Prime Minister, has insisted that we are now a 'classless society'. However, there are indications that market research agencies divide the general public into very clearly defined categories. The Stanford Research Institute (now known as SRI) has recently put together a VALS ('values and lifestyles') matrix consisting of eight categories. These eight categories represent eight different kinds of people whom the adverts of the 1990s will specifically target. These categories, derived through 'psychographic analysis', are as follows:[15]

1. *Actualizers* These are well-informed people who have wide intellectual interests, who are politically active, who emphasise personal growth, who are concerned with social issues, and who enjoy varied leisure activities.
2. *Achievers* These are people whose lives revolve around career and family, who are politically conservative, who are not prone to excessive changes, and who tend to put work before recreation.
3. *Believers* These are people who enjoy a comfortable and somewhat predictable existence, who respect rules and authority figures, and who are likewise politically conservative.
4. *Makers* These are people who prefer 'hands-on' activities, who enjoy the outdoors, who avoid joining organisations (except unions), who distrust politicians and foreigners, and who enjoy leisure with friends and family.
5. *Fulfilleds* These are people for whom leisure centres on the home, who are moderately involved in politics

and the local community, who value education and travel, and who are health-conscious.

6. *Experiencers* These are people who like exercise and socialising, who go for the new and the offbeat, who are politically apathetic, and who are image-conscious and unconforming, whilst admiring wealth and power.

7. *Strivers* These are people who are easily bored, who have narrow interests, who look to their peer group for motivation and approval, who are uninterested in health and nutrition, and who, again, are politically inactive.

8. *Strugglers* These are people whose main concerns are their safety and security, who have restricted activities and interests, and who are conservative and traditional.

It is important for us to recognise that this VALS programme is now far more than a market research project. Its developers see it as a potent social agent for the change of American (and Western) culture. Their mission statement highlights the fact that they exist 'to exert a positive and creative force in the evolution of culture'.[16] If this is so, maybe we are not many years away from the kind of social divisions that we find in *Brave New World*. The only real difference between a world of Alphas, Betas, Gammas, Deltas and Epsilons on the one hand, and Actualizers, Achievers, Believers, Makers, Fulfilleds, Experiencers, Strivers and Strugglers on the other, is the fact that the former is created through eugenics whilst the latter is created through the mass media.

The prevalence of *soma*

A more obvious parallel between *Brave New World* and contemporary culture is the widespread use of narcotics as a means of coping with reality. T. S. Eliot said in *Four Quartets* that 'human kind cannot bear very much reality'. Both Huxley's dystopia and our present society have concocted drugs which assist people to take the edge off reality. In *Brave New World*, the principal drug is of course *soma*. *Soma* is 'euphoric, narcotic, pleasantly hallucinant'. It has 'all the advantages of Christianity and alcohol; none of their side-effects'. It is legal and distributed to citizens at set times in the day and the week so that they can 'take holidays from reality'. As Dr Shaw says, 'Every *soma*-holiday is a bit of what our ancestors used to call eternity.'

In our contemporary culture, there are many equivalents of *soma*. In particular, we should note the appearance of new kinds of prescription drugs which are designed to help people under stress become more self-confident and assured. A recent article in the *Sunday Times* headed 'The feel-good factor' began,

> Imagine it were possible to transform yourself, to change your personality forever. Where once you were shy, now you can be self-confident; where once you sat quietly on the sidelines at parties, now you find yourself the life and soul.
>
> This transformation would be achieved not through the endless reading of self-help books, not even through years of expensive therapy, but simply by the popping of a pill. The question is, would you take one? Would you ask your doctor for a prescription?[17]

Oliver James and Sue Clarke, the authors of the report,

asked this question because of the appearance of a new prescription drug called Prozac. This drug was originally developed as an antidepressant but is now being used more widely because it helps healthy people to become happy, assertive, well adjusted and sociable. It started being prescribed in the USA in 1987 as a replacement for Valium and Librium. Within two years, 650,000 prescriptions of this 'wonder drug' were being handed out each month. By 1993, nine million people around the world had taken Prozac, 500,000 of them in this country. By 1994, the number of people taking Prozac worldwide had risen to 11 million, with annual sales of the drug approaching £1.2 billion. Peter Kramer, who has written a book about Prozac (*Listening to Prozac*[18]), claims that this drug will become even more popular as we evolve into a culture of cosmetic pharmacology – a world where not only noses and breasts can be improved, but emotions and mental states too! Even today it is the best-selling antidepressant in the world.

The *Sunday Times* report on Prozac was quick to spot the similarities with *soma*. James and Clarke described it as 'a younger sister, perhaps, to Aldous Huxley's blissful, dehumanizing *soma* of his novel, *Brave New World*'.[19] The photographs that accompanied the article included a picture of Linda Lysenko playing the part of Lenina Crowne in the film version of *Brave New World*. The report cited a highly critical comment by Professor Ian Hindmarch, head of human pharmacology at Surrey University. He too noticed the similarities with *soma*:

> I find the whole idea of happiness pills and Brave New World drugs appalling. It is our challenge as human beings to cope with the whole range of human emotions, and antidepressants should only be

used for people who are clinically depressed. *Permanent happiness is not a normal human condition.* [Italics mine][20]

It is not clear whether Prozac will become as popular in Britain as it is in the USA. With around five thousand doctors already prescribing the drug (under the brand name Fluoxetine), it is impossible to discard the possibility. Taking a small green-and-white capsule which enhances the work of serotonin, a mood-enhancing chemical in the brain, is likely to become a popular alternative to expensive therapy in a culture suffering from severe malaise, especially when the only side-effect appear to be a reduction in the ability to feel. Indeed, the only thing that is likely to put some people off is the claim that it reduces the ability to experience an orgasm. That may place some, in this erotic culture of ours, in an intolerable dilemma.

So the media are already discerning modern, legal equivalents to *soma*. James and Clarke concluded their perceptive report with the following allusion to Huxley:

> It is all rather reminiscent, in fact, of Huxley's *Brave New World*, where citizens were given *soma* – a pleasantly hallucinogenic recreational drug with no side-effects – to distract them from any of the feelings of unease inherent in the human condition. In the light of the controversy surrounding Prozac, the novel reads like a prophetic warning.[21]

The emergence of a new hedonism

The appearance of *soma*-equivalents highlights more than anything else the worrying parallels between *Brave New*

World and contemporary culture. In this chapter we have looked at a number of important similarities between Huxley's dystopia and our society: the development of eugenics, the threat to family life, the hypnopaedic power of advertising, the appearance of a new class system based on market research, and the first signs of legal equivalents to *soma*. Of all of these it is the appearance of drugs like Prozac that is most worrying, for with Prozac we come face to face with our society's growing preoccupation with hedonism – with finding pleasurable ways of escaping from the stresses and strains of life. However, even Prozac cannot be regarded as the primary means of escape in our culture. That dubious privilege goes to sex, which is increasingly modelled as the main way of taking a holiday from reality. Again, this is a trend that Huxley foresaw in *Brave New World*.

3 NO LEISURE FROM PLEASURE

'Ten to five on the roof this afternoon,' he said,
'as usual.'[1]

One of the most haunting chapters of *Brave New World*
occurs towards the beginning of the novel. It starts with
a deceptive sense of 'paradise regained':

> Outside, in the garden, it was playtime. Naked in
> the warm June sunshine, six or seven hundred little
> boys and girls were running with shrill yells over the
> lawns, or playing ball games, or squatting silently in
> twos and threes among the flowering shrubs. The
> roses were in bloom, two nightingales soliloquized
> in the boskage, a cuckoo was just going out of tune
> among the lime trees. The air was drowsy with the
> murmur of bees and helicopters.[2]

Everything looks idyllic as the Director shows his
students around the garden, where the naked children
play and the birds sing. However, all is not as it seems.
Even in the description above, a discordant note is hinted
at amidst all this apparent harmony (the cuckoo going
out of tune). The next moment, this sense of impending
cacophony is realised as the Director is interrupted by 'a
loud boo-hooing':

> From a neighbouring shrubbery emerged a nurse,

leading by the hand a small boy, who howled as he
went. An anxious-looking little girl trotted at her
heels.

'What's the matter?' asked the Director.

The nurse shrugged her shoulders. 'Nothing
much,' she answered. 'It's just that this little boy
seems rather reluctant to join in the ordinary erotic
play. . . .'[3]

The loss of sexual innocence

This little scene in which naked children are supervised
by nurses in the art of 'erotic play' is fraught with significance. The narrator explains that, 'For a very long period
before the time of Our Ford, and even for some generations afterwards, erotic play between children had been
regarded as abnormal . . . actually immoral'. Now, however, such 'play' was both normal and indeed compulsory.
In a society in which everyone belongs to everyone else,
and where casual sex is therefore normative, children are
conditioned from the earliest age to value eroticism. Like
soma, sex is one of the means advocated by the World
Controllers for taking holidays from reality. For that value
to be ingrained deep within the corporate psyche,
children must be given both sex education and sexual
experience as young as possible.

All this seems frighteningly relevant to contemporary
readers. Consider, for example, the aftermath of an incident in which a nurse was severely reprimanded, following
a visit to a class of 10- and 11-year-olds, for being explicit
about oral sex. The reprimand came from the then Education Secretary, John Patten (incidentally, a committed
evangelical Christian). However, the Government itself

was divided over John Patten's strong indictments, with John Patten's department (Education) at odds with Virginia Bottomley's (Health). At this time, the Department of Health, trying to redress the situation of Britain having the highest number of teenage pregnancies in Europe, was pursuing Mrs Bottomley's approach of teaching schoolchildren about sex and contraception. John Patten expressed his strong disapproval of lessons that might encourage sexual activity amongst children and teenagers.

All this is a symptom of a society in which girls and boys as young as 12 are engaged in sexual relations, and in which nurses at youth centres and schools are therefore forced into giving advice concerning condoms and the like. Some, like John Patten, would prefer to follow the example of some American states and move the emphasis away from graphic explanations towards more traditional teaching on the value of marriage and family life. Whilst this 'sex respect' approach may be something admirable in theory, in practice many children have already lost their sexual innocence by the time they are exposed to slogans like, 'Do the right thing! Wait for the ring!' Indeed, a sadder fact still is the growing awareness that a large number of British children have learnt about sex first-hand from someone abusing them. The truth is, our children know sooner, and they know more. Doling out free contraceptives to children in youth centres is just one step closer to the morality (or amorality) of *Brave New World*.

The condom society

What has happened to British society to make children so sexually aware? In a nutshell, the problem today is that

sex has become a 'value-free' issue. Everywhere the
notion is promoted that we are permitted to give full
expression to our sexual appetites without regard to commitment or consequences. Take as an example the teenage
magazine *More*. An issue in 1992 contained a 16-page
supplement to pull out, called 'Sex: a smart girl's guide'.
Pages 2 and 3 considered the question, 'Can going to bed
with someone too soon spoil the start of a beautiful
relationship?' Pages 4 and 5 contain answers to readers'
letters about enjoying better and safer sex. Nowhere was
the question asked, 'Is sexual intercourse outside marriage
right or wrong?' The assumption throughout the supplement was that smart girls are having sex anyway, so
why not help them to get the best out of what they are
already doing?

What these examples reveal is a paradigm shift in the
way young people view sex. Sex outside marriage is not
considered morally wrong. Biblical morality has now been
replaced by hedonistic amorality. 'If it feels good, then do
it' is the motto. The value is emphasised in particular
through music and film. The following lyrics are not
untypical of what the average youngster listens to every
day:

> In the middle of the night, when the time is right
> Sexily right, I'm gonna do the right thing
> Gonna move you slow, much harder though
> Sexily so. I'm gonna do the right thing
> Feelin' hot, I ain't never gonna stop
> To get what you got . . .[4]

That's from Simply Red's song 'The right thing', from
the album *Men and Women*. It is tame compared with
many of the lyrics in raunchy heavy metal songs, as

Michael Medved has shown in his book, *Hollywood Versus America*.[5] Tame or not, however, the example from Simply Red points to the now blatant promiscuity in contemporary music – a promiscuity that makes the permissiveness of the sixties look relatively innocuous.

But music is not the only means used by mass culture to promote a hedonistic embrace of erotica. Erotic films – which are watched by many young people on their parents' satellite TV networks, and on their own video cassette recorders – also promote this kind of freewheeling 'sexploration'.[6] For example, one of the most controversial films of the decade so far has been *Body of Evidence*, starring Willem Defoe and Madonna. This is a blatantly erotic film. As Uli Edel, the director, was later to report:

> When I first met Madonna, I told her what the erotic scenes would be. She said however far we went, she would go a little bit further.[7]

The leading film magazine *Empire*, when they ran an article on 'Sex in the movies', began with this film as an example of the new permissiveness of the nineties. Simon Witter, who put the piece together, pointed to the use of candle wax and handcuffs in one sex scene. That scene is just the tip of a gratuitously erotic iceberg. Whatever the film's demerits (and they are many), *Body of Evidence* highlights the increasing use of explicit sex as a means of marketing today's movies.

A visit to the feelies

Brave New World anticipated this trend. One of the most powerful chapters of Huxley's novel describes John's one and only visit to 'the feelies' – an interactive cinema in which the spectator can actually feel all the experiences portrayed on screen. The 'feely effects' are achieved by holding onto metal knobs on the arms of the chairs. The film that John and Lenina watch tells the story of an erotic affair between a male Negro and a blonde female. The lights go down, and John and Lenina are plunged into complete darkness:

> Then suddenly, dazzling and incomparably more solid-looking than they would have seemed in actual flesh and blood, far more real than reality, there stood the stereoscopic images, locked in one another's arms, of a gigantic Negro and a golden-haired young brachycephalic Beta-Plus female.[8]

The film begins with these two figures making love on a bearskin rug, 'every hair of which . . . could be separately and distinctly felt'. The narrator describes John's reactions:

> The Savage started. That sensation on his lips! He lifted a hand to his mouth; the titillation ceased; let his hand fall back on the metal knob; it began again. The scent organ, meanwhile, breathed pure musk. Expiring, a sound track super-dove cooed 'Oo-ooh'; and vibrating only thirty-two times a second, a deeper than African bass made answer: 'Aa-aah.' 'Ooh-ah! Ooh-ah!' the stereoscopic lips came together again, and once more the facial erogenous zones of the six thousand spectators in the Alhambra tingled with almost intolerable galvanic pleasure. 'Ooh . . .'[9]

Basic instincts

As ever, Huxley was well ahead of his time. In the 1930s, cinema was not like this at all. The reason for this lay in the inauguration of the Hays Code, named after the US Postmaster General, Will H. Hays. Amongst many other rules, the Hays Code insisted on the legendary 'one-foot-on-the-floor' edict for intertwined couples. 'Excessive and lustful kissing' was banned, along with 'lustful embraces, suggestive postures and gestures'. A fine of $25,000 was slapped on any distributor who infringed these codes of cinematic practice. The effect was that for over thirty years sexually suggestive material was largely absent from films. Even Walt Disney removed a scene in which the seven dwarfs made a bed for Snow White, in case he was criticised for suggesting that they were engaging in something that would make his heroine very far from 'snow white'.

In the 1960s, however, things changed. By the beginning of that decade, the power of the Hays office had severely diminished. After *100 Rifles* was released in 1969, sex in the movies was never the same again. *100 Rifles* contained the first interracial love scene in the history of cinema – Raquel Welch making love to Jim Brown. Huxley's film portraying a sex act between 'a gigantic Negro' and a 'golden-haired young brachycephalic Beta-Plus female' had become a reality. From this moment on, the dreaded Hays C-rating ('Condemned!') became a thing of the past.

Today, of course, we are witnessing a large number of mainstream films which have sought to go as far as possible in the portrayal of explicit sex on screen. Jean-Jacques Annaud's *The Lover*, Uli Edel's *Body of Evidence*, James Foley's *After Dark my Sweet*, Zalman King's *Wild Orchid*, and Adrian Lyne's *9½ Weeks*, *Fatal Attraction* and *Indecent Proposal* – all contain erotic images. Of particular note was Paul Verhoeven's *Basic Instinct*, starring Michael Douglas and Sharon Stone, which told the story of a woman who dispatched her male victims with an ice pick while having sex.

Virtual reality and virtual sex

Mainstream films like these are, however, quite unlike Huxley's feelies in one important sense. Whilst the erotic images of flat-screen movies do arouse people, even with wide-screen and Dolby surround they can only affect our feelings indirectly. However, all this is likely to change in the future. The new technology of 'virtual reality' is likely to be exploited by the pornographic industry, and this could allow the viewer to feel the experiences portrayed on screen. It could make 'the feelies' a reality in everyday, popular culture.

The opening credits of the film called *The Lawnmower Man* provide the following notice:

> By the turn of the millenium a technology known as Virtual Reality will be in widespread use. It will allow you to enter computer-generated artificial worlds as unlimited as the imagination itself. Its creators foresee millions of positive uses – while others fear it as a new form of mind control . . .[10]

In their 1992 book, *Glimpses of Heaven, Visions of Hell*,[11] authors Barrie Sherman and Phil Judkins define virtual reality (VR) as a technology that 'allows you to explore a computer-generated world by actually being in it'. They describe it as 'science fiction come true', or 'science fact'.

They say that the aim of VR creators is to construct a machine that will enable the user to experience what they call 'total immersion' in a three-dimensional virtual world. The basic computer system, known as a 'reality engine', will produce believable graphics and stereo sound, an utterly convincing artificial reality that responds to our every movement. Indeed, they point out that VR will enable us to play God: to control a whole – albeit artificial – reality.

By the end of 1992, the first, very basic virtual-reality machines were being used in arcades and in shops. If you take a trip to Meadowhall here in Sheffield, you will find a shop which sells 'Virtual Reality'. In the centre of that shop there is a cordoned-off area with a VR machine. For £3.00 you are allowed to put on a backpack and headset with the potential for 360-degree vision. Most importantly, you put on a special glove with a hand control. When you turn your head, the graphics on the headset respond accordingly. When you move your hand – say to open a door – the graphics again respond.

From even these very brief comments we can see that virtual reality may well open the door to Huxley's feelies. At present, a full-body 'data-suit' is being designed for the user of VR, complete with 'tactor' (the equivalent of the metal knobs that John held at the feelies). This will enable people who want to participate in 'dildonics', or virtual sex, to experience realistic tactile sensations all over their bodies. Indeed, the entire human body will act as a sensor for a computer system. As Sherman and Judkins wrote:

> This is not the stuff of the Dream Channel, rather it is a logical extension of virtuphone or virtuconference territory. It is also the extension of what will

be virtual dating schemes, which will replace the old computer dating bureaux. It has to be assumed that VR technology will not hold virtual sex back, although the time taken to get into a skin-tight suit dotted with tactile stimulators in the appropriate places will probably preclude any thought of spontaneous love-making, needing as it will the help of considerable amounts of baby powder or oil.[12]

Clearly VR is neutral in itself. It can be used for good as well as evil; it has educational and training value, and already there are signs that it will be used in life-saving surgery. However, many are worried that, like genetics, the technology is advancing too fast for proper moral reflection. As far as sex is concerned, the differences between cinema and VR will be immense. VR is a distinct medium characterised by five I's: intensive, interactive, immersive, illustrative, and intuitive.[13] It is a medium that is likely to use all our concentration and fill all our senses. It will promote active experience of alternative photorealistic bodies which, to use Huxley's words, may feel 'more real than reality'. As such, it has all the potential to create a schizoid society in which people are meeting, touching, buying, talking, working and playing in a virtual world. Those who want to will be able to live the lives of an infinite number of alter egos. Most worrying of all, virtual adultery, not to mention child pornography, could well become commonplace.[14]

The Solidarity Service

The 'feelies' therefore represent one major means of erotic play in *Brave New World*. They are a medium whose modern equivalent is virtual reality. Two other significant media are music and dance, both of which are used erotically in Huxley's novel. Here again there are very noticeable similarities with aspects of popular culture today.

The first example of this sensual use of music technology is in Chapter 5, when Lenina goes to the Westminster Abbey Cabaret. Calvin Stopes and his Sixteen Sexophonists are playing, and they are employing all the latest apparatus for synthetic music. Lenina and Henry (her lover for the night) enter the great domed building where four hundred other couples are already gyrating around the polished floor. The narrator describes the seductive effects of the music:

> The sexophones wailed like melodious cats under the moon, moaned in the alto and tenor registers as though the little death were upon them. Rich with a wealth of harmonics, their tremulous chorus mounted towards a climax, louder and ever louder — until at last, with a wave of his hand, the conductor let loose the final shattering note of ether music and blew the sixteen merely human blowers clean out of existence.[15]

Having taken *soma* before entering, Lenina and Henry dance in another world — 'the warm, the richly coloured, the infinitely friendly world of *soma*-holiday'. Inside Westminster Abbey, they are safe in an environment which has a 'perennially blue sky'. The effects of the *soma*, the lights, and the very latest in 'Synthetic Music apparatus' are to create an impenetrable wall between the actual universe and their minds. As they dance, they become one. Indeed, 'they might have been twin embryos gently rocking together on the waves of a bottled ocean of blood-surrogate'.

In the very next section of *Brave New World*, Bernard Marx goes to a 'Solidarity Service'. After an early dinner, he enters a building in which there are seven thousand rooms set apart for these fortnightly Solidarity Groups. Bernard's is Room 3210 on floor thirty-three. In this room there are twelve chairs around a table:

> Man, woman, man, in a ring of endless alternation round the table. Twelve of them ready to be made one, waiting to come together, to be fused, to lose their twelve separate identities in a larger being.[16]

The President at the meeting stands up and switches on some synthetic music. The 'soft indefatigible beating of drums' ushers in the haunting melody of the first Solidarity Hymn. The pulsing rhythm, accompanied by the *soma* tablets and the 'loving cup of strawberry ice-cream *soma*', creates a haunting atmosphere in which the twelve become one. They all sing:

> Ford, we are twelve; oh, make us one,
>   Like drops within the Social River;
> Oh, make us now together run
>   As swiftly as thy shining Flivver.[17]

A second cup is drunk 'to the Greater Being', and, as the drum beat continues, a second Solidarity Hymn is sung:

> Come, Greater Being, Social Friend,
>   Annihilating Twelve-in-One!
> We long to die, for when we end,
>   Our larger life has but begun.[18]

And so it goes on. Eventually, the service climaxes with all twelve participants singing:

> Orgy-porgy, Ford and fun,
> Kiss the girls and make them One.
> Boys at one with girls at peace;
> Orgy-porgy gives release.[19]

Rave new world

Again, Huxley's words are frighteningly prophetic – this time of the rave culture. Rave music is a combination of Mediterranean disco music and 1970s electronic dance music, which has now been popular for about ten years. Rave parties are held every weekend, and hundreds, sometimes thousands, of young people are attracted to them. Indeed, it is now estimated that each week about one million young people visit a rave. Each time they go, they spend an average of £75 and stay approximately 24 hours. In these parties, the relentless rhythm of up-tempo techno-music, along with the effects of dehydration, ecstasy, lighting, and incitement by disc jockeys to lose oneself in a kind of oceanic oneness, succeed in producing a kind of techno-trance. This trance-like state helps young people to take holidays from the realities which they cannot bear during the week. For this reason the rave culture has touched more under-25s than all the previous youth cults put together.

The similarities with Huxley's Solidarity Services are obvious. First of all, there is the prevalence of the drug ecstasy (and indeed others, such as crack and LSD). Ecstasy, or 'disco biscuits', is closely related to amphetamine (a stimulant), and mescaline (a hallucinogenic).

Interestingly, mescaline was the drug that Huxley argued should be made available on a legal basis to the population. In his book *The Doors of Perception* (1954), Huxley describes how, on one bright morning in 1953, he took four-tenths of a gram of mescaline, sat down and waited to see what happened. Within a couple of hours, his consciousness started to change. He wrote:

> I was seeing what Adam had seen on the morning of his creation – the miracle, moment by moment, of naked existence.[20]

We will return to *The Doors of Perception* later on, but for now we must notice one important fact. Huxley advocated that mescaline should be available legally to all who wanted it, because

> Administered in suitable doses, it changes the quality of consciousness more profoundly and yet is less toxic than any other substance in the pharmacologist's repertory.[21]

Today, ecstasy is fast becoming the illegal equivalent of Huxley's *soma*. It is well known that young people who attend raves also take this designer drug because it produces a state of euphoria and of empathy. It is because the drug produces a sense of empathy – of oneness with others – that ecstasy is taken at raves. By and large, it is not a drug that individuals take on their own.

This desire for empathy between the lost tribes of young people marks a second vital parallel between contemporary rave culture and Huxley's Solidarity Services. All the songs in the Solidarity Service are about the annihilation of individuality:

> Feel how the Greater Being comes!
> Rejoice and, in rejoicing, die!
> Melt in the music of the drums!
> For I am you and you are I.[22]

'Melting in the music of the drums' is a perfect description of what occurs at a rave. At a recent Cyber Punk rave, a reporter heard three DJs shouting in unison:

> We will no longer tolerate individuality. We have no personality, and we don't *want* any personality![23]

Other parallels exist between raves and the Solidarity Services of *Brave New World*. The role of the President in Huxley's rave-equivalents anticipates the key role played by the DJs in raves and their more recent offshoots. But the most important parallel lies in the way both events are intimately related to eroticism.

Huxley evokes a sense of heightened eroticism through various means. The songs have a clearly sexual content, with nouns like 'orgy' and verbs like 'come' figuring prominently. The use of puns like 'sexophonists' to describe the musical instruments clearly highlight the way in which these Huxleyan raves are designed to achieve sexual at-onement between the dancers. Most obvious of all is the remark, made by the narrator in describing the Westminster Abbey Cabaret, that 'Lenina did not forget to take all the contraceptive precautions prescribed by the regulations'.

In contemporary raves, the link between dance and eroticism is equally obvious. One 24-year-old man described the first experience of taking ecstasy, at a London nightclub, in words that are overtly sexual:

> I'd heard so much about it that I couldn't wait to

try it myself. Friends had said that it would taste disgusting and it did. They also said that I'd experience the most wonderful feelings of warmth and euphoria. They were right. The first pill was like nothing on earth. I felt wonderful, all happy and relaxed, and every now and again I'd get this wonderful whooshing feeling all over my body like an orgasm. The next day I ached a bit from having danced all night, but I didn't feel any ill-effects.[24]

The link between the euphoric effects of ecstasy and the moment of orgasm is clearly sexual. But the link does not end here. We should also note the way in which raves encourage – as a result of experiences of momentary at-onement, community and empathy – casual sex. The problem, of course, is that relationships that begin at a rave usually turn out to be false relationships. Thus one person said of the first year of nightclubs and ecstasy:

I made untold mistakes during that year, massive misjudgements about relationships. I was getting into one false relationship after another with completely unsuitable girls. I saw the same happening with nice girls that I knew were taking it. They ended up with low-life losers, because they founded their relationships on an evening of Ecstasy when everything looked rosy and loving and perfect. They still hold that shared memory dear to them even though they can never achieve those initial feelings again.[25]

The gospel of sexual hedonism

In the final analysis, what Huxley foresaw was the widespread recourse to sex as just one means (perhaps the major means) of taking a holiday from reality. What I believe he did not predict is the apotheosis of Eros into an actual religion, an apotheosis clearly indicated by the popularity of Madonna. Even Huxley did not see that sex would eventually become an object of worship. Indeed, in 1952 he wrote as follows:

> Like intoxication, elementary sexuality, indulged in for its own sake and divorced from love, was once a god, worshipped not only as the principle of fertility, but also as a manifestation of the radical otherness immanent in every human person. *In theory, elementary sexuality has long ceased to be a god.* [Italics mine][26]

Today I am not sure Huxley would have written those words, for the evidence is all around us that eroticism has become an idol in our contemporary society. To take just one example: one day I caught a pop video being shown on children's TV. It portrayed a monk in a red habit in a monastery setting, and the music sounded like Gregorian chant imposed on top of dance music. The track was called 'Sadness'. I went out to the shops and bought the album of the same name, by the band Enigma. On returning home, I discovered that 'Sadness' was actually a pun for 'Sade-ness' (as in the Marquis de Sade, a figure associated with sexual excesses, particularly sadomasochism). The inside sleeve also contained this quotation from Sigmund Freud:

> The pleasure of satisfying a savage instinct, undomesticated by the ego, is incomparably much more intense than the one of satisfying a tamed instinct. Reason is becoming the enemy that prevents us from a lot of possibilities of pleasure.

Further investigation revealed that Christian worship

(Gregorian chant) was being used to promote the expression of basic sexual instincts; sex was being marketed as a religion. Let us therefore keep in mind the fact that there are differences as well as similarities between popular culture and *Brave New World*. In some ways our situation is better, but in others it is far worse. In the next chapter, we will begin to answer the question, 'Why?'

4 CHRISTIANITY WITHOUT TEARS

'Christianity without tears – that's what *soma* is.'[1]

Why *is* our society becoming so like Aldous Huxley's *Brave New World*? Why are we increasingly becoming a people who are, to use Neil Postman's well-known phrase, 'amusing ourselves to death'?

In 1987 Anne Wilson Schaef produced a remarkable and highly influential book, *When Society Becomes an Addict*.[2] Schaef's is an immensely important book which helps to explain *why* we are what we have become – an addictive society.

The key concept of addiction

Central to Schaef's thesis is the proposition that society has developed all the characteristics of an addict. That being the case, we need to start with a definition of addiction.

The word 'addiction' used to be employed purely in the context of habitual drug-taking, but now has a usage far beyond that. Today people may be said to have an addiction to anything from shopping to jogging. The word 'addiction' comes from the Latin verb *addicere*, which means 'to hand over' or 'to surrender'. This suggests that an addiction is something to which I surrender, something to which my life is given over. That indeed is the case: addicts are people who have lost control of their lives and who are now controlled by their addiction – alcohol, gambling, sport, cleaning, drugs, whatever. Addicts are people whose lives have become unmanageable as a result of their excessive attachment to someone or to something.

The reason why we become addicted is that the objects of attachment have an alluring, anaesthetic quality about them. They alter our moods. They anaesthetise us to the harsh realities of life. The problem is, however, that ultimately they are never enough. The experience of addiction is like drinking sea water: the more you drink, the thirstier you become. Addictions are always progressive: we become more and more obsessive, more and more dependent, more and more deceived, and more and more destructive. Denial sets in as the attachment strengthens. We lie to ourselves and to others. 'I could give up tomorrow,' we claim. Even the evidence of loved ones getting hurt as a result of our addictions is often not enough to produce the awakening that may lead to recovery. The power of the anaesthetic is too great, the need to take that holiday from reality too strong. Instead of dealing with the pain within, we take no leisure from seeking pleasure. The reason? At the end of the day, 'human kind cannot bear very much reality'.

Addiction can therefore be defined as *an attachment to a mood-altering agent that is excessive and destructive, leading to feelings of powerlessness and eventually to 'hitting bottom'.*

The root of addiction

If we are to understand how we become addicted, we must understand the root of addiction. What lies at the heart of addiction? What lies at the root of such dependence? The answer, in a word, is pain. Pain is where the process of addiction begins. When we feel pain, we quite instinctively look for an anaesthetic. In today's climate, in which pain relievers have become best-selling products, the opportunities for pain relief have greatly multiplied. The means of relief are now more varied, more accessible, more widespread than ever before. The problem is, however, that our society has become less able to distinguish between the kinds of pain that it is legitimate to anaesthetise (such as arthritic aches, migraine, and so on), and the kinds of pain that really need to be confronted and dealt with. In our society, the denial of all forms of pain seems to have become an accepted and even desirable ethic in our collective, unwritten, value system.

In reality, of course, there are different sorts of pain. The most fundamental kind is of a spiritual nature, and this kind of pain needs to be faced rather than masked. In a key article entitled 'Philosophical-religious factors in the etiology and treatment of alcoholism',[3] Dr Howard Clinebell identifies the primary pain behind alcohol addiction as spiritual in nature. In fact, he describes alcoholism as the attempt to fulfil religious needs through pseudo-religious means – to find God in a bottle. The primary need we all have, Clinebell proposes, is the need for a sense of meaning and purpose in life. We live daily with the knowledge that we are mortal and that one day we shall die. This knowledge produces a deep sense of unease, which Clinebell calls 'existential anxiety'. This is another term for what Erik Erikson called the 'ego chill',

Paul Tillich 'man's essential loneliness', and Albert Camus 'the sense of alienation'. At the root of human awareness is the desire for someone or something that will fill the hole in the soul. If the Churches do not provide an answer, Clinebell contends, then people will look elsewhere to remove this most fundamental pain of all. They will look to addictions.

Spiritual pain is one form of pain that needs to be faced rather than erased. Often there are other kinds of pain that need to be confronted as well. There is emotional pain – for example, the pain of living in poverty or solitude; the pain of never having known a father, or of having had a father who was emotionally absent, or a father who abused; the pain of some dreadful trauma, such as a car crash or a house fire; the ongoing pain of depression; and the pain of low self-esteem. Pain lies at the heart of most addictions. Some addictions derive from 'appetitive' motives – they derive, that is, from an appetite for pleasurable effects. Most addictions, however, derive from 'escape-avoidance' motivation. People seek out pleasurable sensations that enable them to experience temporary relief from the pain within. Pain, then, and particularly existential anxiety or spiritual pain, lies at the heart and at the root of addiction.

The process of addiction

What happens when pain is registered? Once pain becomes apparent, many people reach out to an addictive agent – such as gambling, sex, work, alcohol, or dependent relationships – in order to mask the pain. This results in a kind of temporary anaesthesia: addictions actually dull pain. Through certain forms of mood-altering activity, people actually produce a pain-relieving change in the chemistry of their brains. Enkephalins, and related compounds known as endorphins, are released during eating, exercise, smoking, drinking alcohol, and the like. These compounds are similar to opiate drugs; they are, as it were, nature's pain-relievers. No wonder addictions are, on the surface, such an attractive option: they offer people temporary anaesthesia.

The process of addiction, however, is progressive and destructive. The euphoric experience of taking a holiday from reality becomes the all-consuming goal of a person's life. It is not long, therefore, before an obsessive and dependent attachment to the addictive agent sets in. If the process is left unchecked, then a person usually ends up 'hitting bottom'. She or he may experience a health

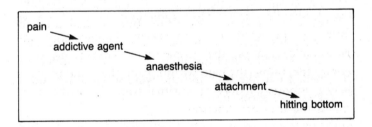

crisis, a marriage break-up, redundancy, financial ruin, or something of the sort. This in turn may precipitate an awakening which leads to recovery (usually through a Twelve-Step Recovery programme, as we will see later), but this does not always happen. Instead, the process of addiction may end in death – the drug addict who over-doses herself, the adrenalin junkie who takes one risk too many, the workaholic who drives himself to a heart attack. The overall process of addition (see above) is therefore a slippery slope, beginning with pain and ending in more pain.

An example of addiction

In a recent issue of the magazine *Options*, the following story was related by Kathy, a 29-year-old teacher. Her sad tale provides a helpful example of the process of addiction, in this case sex addiction. It begins with an identification of the pain that lay at the core of her obsessive behaviour. In this instance, the pain was the feeling of dirtiness caused by her father's behaviour towards her when she was a child:

> I was programmed for sex addiction. No one taught me about my body. I was never told about periods, or where babies come from. But my dad used to share his secrets with me. He'd tell me about his affairs and he kept his 'little stash' of porn under my bed. I felt like him and me were so close because I knew all about him.[4]

In the next stage of the story, Kathy identifies the addictive agent she began to use in order to alleviate the pain of her father's behaviour:

> Most of my adolescence I was lost in fantasy. I felt so empty inside, like there was this great big hole, and I used sex to fill it up. All of the girls in high school daydreamed and dated. I just started a little younger and went a little further.[5]

Sex was the addictive agent Kathy used to gain for herself

temporary anaesthesia. Soon a compulsive attachment to sex developed:

> As I got older, it got more obvious that I was different. The other girls started settling down. I just went on having sex with any man that would have me ... I did all sorts of cold ritualised stuff in relationships which left me feeling like trash. I've let men tie me up and beat me even though I felt scared and trapped and hated the pain. I've let them reduce me to some bit part in their sado-masochistic fantasies because I thought that the more extreme their sexual desire the more they loved me. And then they'd leave me and I'd feel used and abandoned, and I'd start bingeing again, going to bars night after night.[6]

Eventually, sexual bingeing inevitably led to the experience of 'hitting bottom':

> I remember when I hit bottom. I was on a real binge of bars. I caught VD for the 12th time. I know it sounds crazy, but I was glad I was sick ... It give me time to think, and I realised what a mess my life was. Work was suffering because I was either exhausted from the night before or I was planning the night to come, or both. I had no girlfriends ...[7]

Kathy's story highlights the process of addiction. In her own story she reveals how it all began with the pain of 'love hunger'. She realised her life was in a mess, and started attending SAA (a Sexaholics Anonymous group). During that time she came to see that every time she had sex she was reliving how she had felt when her dad showed her his pornographic magazines. She came to terms with her real feelings and began to learn to control her sexuality (as opposed to being controlled by it). She ends her story thus:

> I still find it hard sometimes to know what I'm feeling but I can feel myself growing. It's like my sexuality has stopped rushing on ahead and I'm getting my breath back. I hope that, one day, we'll be able to walk at the same pace, still holding hands.[8]

The kinds of addiction

Kathy's story is an example of the way in which sex can become the organising principle of a person's daily life. But sex is just one of the vast number of anaesthetics that are freely available today. Hemfelt and Fowler, in their work amongst addicts,[9] have identified the following addictive agents:

1. Alcohol and drugs.
2. Work, achievement, and success.
3. Money addictions, such as overspending, gambling, hoarding.
4. Control addictions.
5. Food addictions.
6. Sexual addictions.
7. Approval dependency (the need to please people).
8. Rescuing patterns.
9. Dependency on toxic relationships.
10. Physical illness (hypochondria).
11. Exercise and physical conditioning.
12. Cosmetics, clothes, cosmetic surgery, trying to look good on the outside.
13. Academic pursuits and excessive intellectualising.
14. Religiosity or religious legalism.

15. General perfectionism.
16. Cleaning and avoiding contamination, and other obsessive-compulsive symptoms.
17. Organising, structuring (the need always to have everything in its place).
18. Materialism.

In my own work on addiction, I have organised the many different kinds of mood-altering agents into the following categories: ingestive addictions; process addictions; technological addictions; people addictions; and ideological addictions.

Ingestive addictions

An ingestive addiction is one that involves taking a substance into the body, through the mouth or the nose, or into a vein using a syringe.

The most obvious such addiction is drug addiction. All the signs are that there is currently a huge increase in illegal drug-taking. In November 1991 the *Guardian* reported that, in the first six months, there had been an increase of 25 per cent in the amount of drugs seized at three British airports. These drugs were being flown in from Europe, the Caribbean, South America, West Africa and the Middle East. They included massive quantities of cocaine and heroin. The graphs on page 72 highlight this increase.[10]

These statistics could reflect an increase in police activity rather than an increase in drug smuggling. However, the opinion of the experts is that it reflects both. There is no doubt that certain drugs have become more popular and more available. LSD, for example – the hallucinogenic drug associated with sixties' psychedelia – has

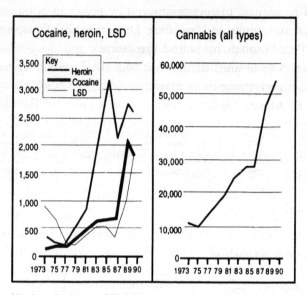

Number of seizures of illegal drugs by police and Customs and Excise in the UK

captured a whole new generation. LSD (lysergic acid diethylamide), 'acid', was seen in the sixties as an exotic drug which enabled users to enjoy a mind-bending trip into the secrets of the universe. Now, in the nineties, LSD has made a big comeback. Today it is regarded by many as a cheap alternative to other drugs connected with the rave culture. At between £4.00 and £5.00 a dose it is much more affordable than many drugs. Not surprisingly, police are fearful that LSD is being particularly targeted at children and young people. Indeed, dealers trafficking in LSD now market tablets with images of cartoon characters such as Batman.

LSD is not the only drug that has dramatically increased in availability and usage. Crack, the highly addictive cocaine derivative, is spreading right across Britain. This drug, hitherto associated with deprived inner-city areas, is now regularly being discovered by police in commuter areas and county towns. One Detective Chief Inspector in Peterborough has stated that 'Crack and drug-related violence is happening in America, in London, and, as with many crimes, it is now following close behind into the provinces.' Dr Brian Wells, of the Centre for Research on Drugs and Health Behaviour, in London, has also warned: 'Seizures are way up. Street prices are falling. The number of cocaine-related deaths has increased. Everything points to the fact that crack is about to become a vast public health and social problem.'

The popularity of crack is connected with the experiences it induces. Crack is cocaine converted into a form that can be smoked rather than injected, swallowed or sniffed. The effects of smoking are different. As Larry Collins explains:

> The smoked cocaine is absorbed not by the membranes lining the nose but by the entire surface of the lungs ... As a result, smoked cocaine bursts through the bloodstream to the heart and on to the brain with a speed and a force so overwhelming that there are no neurological instruments that can even begin to measure its effects.[11]

Smoking crack produces an immediate sense of euphoria which lasts for only a few seconds (forty at the most). That is nothing compared to the 20- or 30-minute high induced by sniffing cocaine. However, it is the *intensity* of the high that makes smoking crack so attractive, which is why crack users become hooked after only two or three times (as opposed to the average of 18 months that it takes to become addicted to cocaine). Nothing compares with the intensity of crack-stimulated highs.

Many other drugs are widespread, including speed, can-

nabis, heroin, magic mushrooms, solvents and tranquillisers, but one in particular deserves specific mention.
Ecstasy – also known as XTC, E, X, and disco biscuits –
is the common name for the drug 3,4-methylenedioxy-
methylamphetamine, or MDMA. It is closely related to
amphetamine (a stimulant) and mescaline (a
hallucinogenic). With its promise of euphoria, it is hardly
surprising that ecstasy has become so popular, with an
estimated 500,000 users in Britain today (compared to
the 150,000–200,000 cocaine users). It is the designer
drug *par excellence*. As Fiona Lafferty puts it:

> It is to the Nineties what cocaine was to the Eighties.
> Ecstasy goes to all the best-dressed parties. It is there
> tucked away in briefcases in the expensively designed
> offices of advertising agencies. No stranger to first
> nights, it is there in the green rooms of theatres,
> ready for when the applause has died down. And,
> most famously, it is there at raves, the all-night parties
> where hundreds of teenagers gather to dance the
> night away.[12]

LSD, crack, ecstasy – all these show worrying signs of
becoming widespread addictions. But they are not the
only common ingestive addictions in contemporary
society. Many legal prescription drugs are also habit-
forming and mood-altering (as in the case of Prozac – see
Chapter 2). The lure of nicotine, too, is still as powerful as
ever. Indeed, a new cigarette known as 'Express' is being
developed which will satisfy the smoker's craving for nicotine in half the time. Caffeine remains popular; tea and
coffee shops – where 'users' can buy and often drink the
most exotic brands – are becoming more and more popular, particularly in the big shopping malls. Food addictions
are becoming more and more prevalent, so much so that

Overeaters Anonymous groups have been started in many areas. Then, of course, there is alcohol. Even school-children are resorting to alcohol. The statistics below reveal that tens of thousands of youngsters are drinking the equivalent of a pint and a half of beer every day:[13]

How much schoolchildren drink in a week					
Amount drunk[1]	Aged 11	Aged 12	Aged 13	Aged 14	Aged 15
None:	75.7%	64.1%	56.7%	44.7%	31.4%
1–6 units:	20.0%	29.0%	29.7%	34.2%	38.8%
7–10 units:	1.7%	3.5%	5.4%	8.8%	12.3%
11–14 units:	1.6%	1.4%	3.7%	5.2%	5.4%
15–20 units:	0.7%	1.0%	2.1%	3.8%	4.6%
21+ units:	0.3%	1.0%	2.4%	3.3%	7.5%

[1]one unit = ½ pint beer/one glass wine/one measure spirit. Source: Schools Health Education Unit, Exeter University.

We will return to the important subject of alcohol later, but the point I want to make here is that ingestive addictions are ubiquitous and that they are increasing. Even the elderly are turning to them. During 1994 there were a number of stories in the newspapers concerning retired people who grow and smoke cannabis. Some people suffering from arthritis have discovered that cannabis is an effective painkiller! Addiction, therefore, crosses all social and generational boundaries. Though the effects of addiction are destructive, people of all walks of life seem more and more prepared to pay the price.

Process addictions

The second kind of addiction that is widespread today may be defined as process addiction. Schaef states that 'In a process addiction one becomes hooked on a process – a specific series of actions or interactions'.[14] Schaef points out that almost any process can become an addictive agent. She cites the following as examples: accumulating money, gambling, sex, work, religion, worry. That, of course, is a far from complete list; there are many other process addictions besides these. In what follows I will briefly highlight some of the more popular ones today.

The most obvious is shopping. A recent survey has revealed that nearly one in six people is addicted to shopping. The Mintel Poll in question found that shoppers fell into five categories or types: addicted, happy, purposeful, reluctant, and obstinate! Addicts (the first type) shop at every opportunity, even if they have nothing in mind to buy. Mintel concluded that 'shopping, or at least window-shopping, has become a national pastime'. In days to come, the attraction of shopping is bound to be exploited even more. Indeed, it is expected that supermarkets will allure us through the use of smells (such as the scent of coconut oil as you pass the suntan lotion) and video-trolleys (small trolley-mounted screens which will seek to persuade consumers by displaying enticing images). These and other technologies will be used to make the *experience* of shopping more addictive than ever.

Another contemporary addiction is to danger. This is adrenalin addiction, and those who are hooked are known as 'adrenalin junkies'. During 1994 a number of teenagers were killed at fairgrounds, and one middle-aged man died of a heart attack after taking a ride on 'Nemesis', a new attraction at Alton Towers. When two teenagers were asked by a reporter in a television interview why they continued to embrace such experiences, they replied that they were 'white-knuckle junkies'. 'If it's dangerous, or at least it seems like that, we love it. We like being frightened, the feeling of being pushed to the edge.' This kind of adrenalin addiction is also manifested in the new, disturbing habit of 'train surfing' (clinging precariously to the outside of train doors). Riding the rails – like going on dangerous rides at the new theme parks – is a way of getting kicks and attracting the admiration of friends.

Just as alarming is the growing addiction to violence. Juvenile crime, particularly gang warfare, is no longer confined to the mean streets of urban priority areas. It is now almost as rife in the leafy suburbs and in rural areas. As Fiona Webster recently reported:

> Crime used to be a hazard that happened to other people, in big cities, and gangs were something you associated with Manchester's Moss Side and London's East End. Now, recent figures reveal that rural crime is on the increase, and a spate of senseless attacks on lone young people in such places as Eton and Hampstead show that the gang is alive and kicking far from the inner-city.[15]

Where unemployment and boredom seem inescapable, violence and other forms of crime quickly turn into addictions. The thrill of the kill, the bonding between fellow addicts, the excitement of the chase – all these combine to make crime an escape from the drab pessimism of life. Twoccing – 'twoc' stands for 'taking without owner's consent', typically cars – is particularly popular. Crime has become one of the primary process addictions in our society today. Indeed, Beatrix Campbell (in her book *Goliath: Britain's Dangerous Places*[16]) suggests that the lawless urban hinterlands of North America will soon be paralleled in Britain.

Shopping, danger, violence – these are just a few of the more visible process addictions in our society at present. Others are music, raves, weekend tripping, holidays, fantasy, driving cars, buying houses, cleaning, perfection- ism, success, power, fashion, beauty, cosmetics, sport, and fitness.

Technological addictions

A technological addiction is an excessive attachment to any aspect of what has been called the 'techno-boom': the result of the digital revolution in computing and communication, and the huge advances in silicon-chip, satellite, ratio and optical-fibre technology. Until relatively recently, these advances mainly affected the workplace, but increasingly the technology is also affecting the home. Virtual-reality machines have been designed for young people who, from as early as five years of age, become expert players of computer games. HDTV (high- definition television), with a wide screen, Dolby surround sound and opportunities for active rather than passive viewing (as with interactive video), is available already in the shops. CD-ROMs – compact discs for TV and home computers, with an emphasis on interaction – are also in people's homes, as are laser-disc films for home cinema entertainment. Nicam stereo is already with us; so are fax machines and mobile phones. Thirty million people in Britain are already using computer modems to tune into the global information 'superhighway' known in some circles as 'cyberspace'. Video telephones are now available; so are highly developed, conveniently-sized personal digi- tal diaries.

There is much that is positive in all of this, but the downside is the fact that the techno-boom makes possible a whole range of accessible and highly attractive addic- tions. Consider two characters who, whilst stereotypes, are representative examples of the 'techno-junkie': the 'Superbrat' and the 'Cyberdude'.

Superbrats are children of the 1990s. Aged between 15 and 24, they care little about the social rights of other people. They live in their own worlds, which they experience as a continuous present. They cruise around in £90 trainers, wearing expensive personal stereo systems (compact disc, of course), quaffing drinks from polystyrene containers and eating fast food. They each have their own TV and VCR, in a bedroom which also contains a computer system (mostly used for violent video games). They may fax homework to each other on their parents' fax machines. They are unashamed materialists. Indeed, from the age of 12, Superbrats have luxuries for which many of today's adults had to wait until they were 30. Their philosophy is described by the media as 'grabbitism'. They are, for the most part, self-orientated gadget addicts. They are committed consumers in a society of free-market affluence.

The second kind of techno-junkie, who is most often male, is the Cyberdude. The Cyberdude is a style-conscious data-dandy who makes regular cybernautical trips into cyberspace. He sports a laptop computer and a portable phone, and is anti-conformist. Marcus Brill writes:

> His preferred style includes surf T-shirts, long baggy shorts and a Silicon Valley pony-tail. The hippest Cyberdudes have systems such as the little Apple Newton, which has a screen that recognizes its owner's hand-writing.[17]

At the moment, many Cyberdudes are in their late twenties. If they live in London, they attend the Virtuali Tearoom where clubbers can bring their own computers, plug into Internet, and go 'Net surfing'. Cyberdudes, so precisely predicted by Bill Gibson in his novel *Neuromancer* (1983), have a motto: it is E. M. Forster's 'only connect'. In an issue of the magazine *CompuServe* entitled 'All things cyber', various writers contributed to make the point that 'More and more, *cyber* is becoming the prefix of the '90s.' Cyberdudes, the *aficionados* of cyberjargon, are communication addicts, and they are here to stay.

The Superbrat and the Cyberdude are examples of what Aldous Huxley called 'technological idolatry'. Technological idolaters, wrote Huxley, 'believe that their redemption and liberation depend upon material objects, namely machines and gadgets'.[18] Not everyone who uses this new technology, of course, is an idolater. Nevertheless, as we experience the massive cultural transition from what has been called the Industrial Age to what we can call the Information Age, excessive attachment to any aspect of this techno-boom constitutes an addiction.

People addictions

A fourth class of addictions includes various forms of relationship addiction. There is already a vast number of books dealing with this area of addictionology.

Most people who write on this particular topic follow Anne Wilson Schaef who, in her book *Escape from Intimacy*,[19] divides people addictions into three categories: sex, romance and relationship addictions. 'It is my experience', Schaef writes, 'that sex, romance, and relationship addictions are *separate* addictions'.[20] The first of these is 'an obsession and preoccupation with sex, in which everything is defined sexually or in terms of sexuality and all perceptions and relationships are sexualised'. Sexual addiction, Schaef argues, is of epidemic proportions and is overtly encouraged by our culture. Perhaps the most poignant example of our culture's obsessive and excessive dependence on sex is the recent behaviour known as 'autoerotic asphyxia'. Schaef takes up the story:

> The idea is to shut off one's oxygen supply, usually by a form of hanging with a rope, while masturbating or having sexual relations. The result is supposed to be a dramatic effect at the point of orgasm or an intensifying of the orgasm. It appears that many more teen suicides than were once expected are related to this form of sexual acting out.[21]

If sexual addiction is disturbing, so is romance addiction. Romance addicts are people who are simply in love with the feeling of being in love (as they understand it). They are addicted to the *idea* of romance. They are addicted to the thrill and the danger of the new romance. They are people who live in a world of illusion, and who are hooked on the intoxicating feeling of romantic fantasy. Many romance addicts feed their craving with real relationships. Others become addicted to romantic fiction (such as that published by Mills and Boon) and to TV soap operas. Others may become obsessed with the picture of a total stranger – with the painting of a romantic beauty, a poster of a film star, or a photograph of a model in a magazine. Others are quite content to live in their own imaginations, feeding on a kind of alternative, inner reality. The forms of romance addiction are many and varied; all forms, however, begin by offering relief but end by inflicting pain.

Relationship addiction is also a form of people addiction. Relationship addiction is a form of emotional terrorism. It is one person's obsession with the idea of having, or the fact of having, a relationship with a particular person. It is the kind of obsession played out by the actress

Glenn Close in the film *Fatal Attraction*. Lori Rentzel
describes this kind of addiction as a dependent relationship, and notes the following signs of such dependency:

> when either party in a relationship
> - experiences frequent jealousy, possessiveness and
>   a desire for exclusivism, viewing other people as a
>   threat to the relationship;
> - prefers to spend time alone with this friend and
>   becomes frustrated when this does not happen;
> - becomes irrationally angry or depressed when this
>   friend withdraws slightly;
> - loses interest in friendships other than this one;
> - experiences romantic or sexual feelings leading to
>   fantasy about this person;
> - becomes preoccupied with this person's appear-
>   ance, personality, problems and interests;
> - is unwilling to make short or long range plans
>   that do not include the other person;
> - is unable to see the other's faults realistically;
> - becomes defensive about the relationship when
>   asked about it;
> - displays physical affection beyond that which is
>   appropriate for a friendship;
> - refers frequently to the other in conversation; feels
>   free to 'speak for' the other;
> - exhibits an intimacy and familiarity with this
>   friend that causes others to feel uncomfortable or
>   embarrassed in their presence.[22]

Sex, romance and relationship addictions have, to use
Schaef's word, reached 'epidemic' proportions today. One
reason for this is that we live in a society in which these
three addictions are being culturally learned all the time,

particularly through the mass media. This is a point well made by Dr Susan Forward in her book, paradoxically entitled *Obsessive Love*:

> Compared to obsession, all other love seems humdrum and mundane. Obsessive love appears to be a sultry, seductive world of heightened emotionality and transcendent sexuality. Movies, television, advertisements, popular songs – they all collude to persuade us that love is not real unless it is all-consuming.[23]

That is certainly true. From adverts for the perfume called 'Obsession' to films like *Basic Instinct*, the mass media technologies of today attempt to persuade us that obsessive, passionate love is the ultimate 'high'. Schaef is right: we live in a society which encourages people addictions.

Ideological addictions

The final category of addictions comprises excessive and mood-altering fixations to ideologies. Most ideologies have the power to become addictive, and most of them are 'isms' – capitalism, Communism, patriotism, socialism, vegetarianism, militarism, paganism, classism, racism, ageism, and so on. An ideological addiction is an excessive attachment to some general idea or cause. The addictive allure of these ideologies has a lot to do with their ability to gather us into communities of fellow-addicts, and with their capacity to explain away the nastier aspects of life with reference to an apparently larger good. A study of ethnic nationalism – a cultural addiction evident for example in the former Yugoslavia – would bear this out.

The most powerful ideological addiction in our society is, of course, consumerism. In his book *Consumer Culture*

and Postmodernism,[24] Mike Featherstone argues eloquently
that consumerism is now central to our understanding of
society. Our society has become a consumer culture in
two senses: firstly, in the sense that buying has become not
only a functional activity but a leisure pursuit; secondly, in
the sense that our culture now depends upon economic
principles of consumption. In the first sense, many aspects
of society encourage us to buy goods for prestige, in order
to identify oneself with a chosen style, and not just as
utilities. The modern consumer is therefore persuaded to
use clothes, home, furniture, decorations and cars as symbols or communicators. In the second sense, there is now
an economy of consumer goods, an economy depending
on supply, demand, competition, and the rest. From the
perspective of classical economics, the object of all pro-
duction is consumption. In this respect, we have sub-
scribed to the consumer values of *Brave New World*:
'Ending is better than mending' and 'The more stitches,
the less riches'.

The drive to accumulate goods is widespread, and the
consumer culture has created an economy to feed this
need. The culture has therefore become fundamentally
hedonistic or 'pleasure-orientated'. People work by day
like Puritans, then relax at night like playboys. Today, says
Featherstone, we live in 'a hedonistic consumer culture
landscape':

> Consumer culture uses images, signs and symbolic
> goods which summon up dreams, desires and fan-
> tasies which suggest romantic authenticity and
> emotional fulfilment in narcissistically pleasing one-
> self, instead of others.[25]

The most obvious sign of this is the creation of the
shopping malls. These pander to the addictive power

of shopping. They beautify ordinary life into dream worlds where it never rains. They are places in which fluid groups of people experience intense moments of empathy and affectual immediacy. In such a Disney World as this, the dividing line between simulation and reality becomes almost invisible. A disturbing example of the consequences of this, drawn from another context, was the answer given by a US fighter pilot on returning from a bombing mission in Iraq during the Gulf War. When a reporter asked what it was like, the pilot replied, 'Very realistic.'

When Society Becomes an Addict

Why has contemporary society become so like the dystopia of Huxley's *Brave New World*? Anne Wilson Schaef's answer might be this: because we have evolved into an addictive society. Schaef understands the phrase 'addictive society' in two senses. First of all, she proposes that society as a whole has taken on the characteristics of an addict. (We will look more closely at this primary connotation later.) Secondly, she proposes that the whole of society is now shot through with the kinds of addiction I have tried to describe in this chapter. The five categories I have discussed – ingestive, process, technological, people, and ideological addictions – are not watertight compartments. Various addictions cross the boundaries: an obsession with 'cybersex', for example, links both technological and people addictions in one behaviour pattern. However, the categories do help to highlight the variety and the ubiquity of addictions in today's society – a variety far greater even than Huxley envisaged. For Huxley himself later commented:

> In the Brave New World of my fables there was no
> whisky, no tobacco, no illicit heroin, no bootlegged
> cocaine. People neither smoked, nor drank, nor sniff-
> ed, nor gave themselves injections. Whenever
> anyone felt depressed or below par he would swallow
> a tablet or two of a chemical compound called
> Soma.[26]

In truth, there are a number of reasons why contemporary society is becoming like 'the Brave New Worldian
nightmare' (and, in some respects, worse). One reason is
provided by sociologists of leisure. They argue that the
addictive society is the result of a combination of a market
economy, affluence, and more time away from work. As
leisure time has increased for many people, vicarious
experiences have been developed to form a central part
of our leisure experience. Vicarious experiences of leisure
are those in which the individual is passively entertained
– watching sport on TV, for example, or taking drugs or
drinking alcohol. In a context in which vicarious leisure
experiences are marketed, addiction is bound to be rife.

Another explanation is proposed by those sociologists
who believe in what are called 'conflict theories'. Kelly
and Godby write:

> Conflict theories of society would explain the
> emergence of a mass entertainment industry and of
> a drug culture as an important method by which
> those in power keep those who might threaten them
> from taking action.[27]

This theory, interestingly, finds many echoes in Huxley's
own discussions concerning *Brave New World*. He too
argued that the creation of an addictive society is an

effective means by which politicians can divert the public from action. In *Brave New World Revisited* he revealed that

> In *Brave New World* non-stop distractions of the most fascinating nature (the feelies, orgy-porgy, centrifugal bumble-puppy) are deliberately used as instruments of policy, for the purpose of preventing people from paying too much attention to the realities of the social and political situation.[28]

Conflict theorists would therefore say that opium is the religion of the people. Pleasurable addictions keep us from political action.

Another reason for the addictive society comes from experts on the family. Many argue that addictive lifestyles are developed as a means of masking the pain caused by a dysfunctional family. Many regard addictions as symptoms of deeper wounds experienced during childhood. Childhood victims of abuse often end up as addicts. Growing up with an addicted parent (such as an alcoholic father), experiencing the death of a parent during one's childhood, having unhealthy gender role models, the experience of rejection (say, through adoption), poor communication in the family, a lack of intimacy – such experiences can often give rise to pain which eventually initiates the process of addiction. It has become quite fashionable to trace every ill back to a dysfunctional family root; yet much of my own experience in the counselling ministry is consistent with the claim that this is indeed a common reason for addiction. In a society like ours, in which happy families are increasingly a thing of the past (as in *Brave New World*), many addictive lifestyles are symptoms of childhood pain.

In the final analysis, however, the emergence of our addictive society cannot be explained away using purely sociological and biochemical reasons. Huxley, later on in his life, came to see that the primary reason for the evolution of such a culture is spiritual, not sociological. In the final chapter of *O Brave New Church* I will suggest that the emergence of a hedonistic society is ultimately a spiritual problem requiring a spiritual solution. That spiritual solution is God's alternative community, his brave new Church.

5 BRAVE NEW CHURCH

'If you allowed yourselves to think of God, you wouldn't allow yourselves to be degraded by pleasant vices. You'd have a reason for bearing things patiently, for doing things with courage.'[1]

In 1991, I caught the following interview between a BBC1 interviewer and the singer Alison Moyet. Her words are, in many ways, a sign of the times:

INTERVIEWER Do you think you are an exaggerated person?

ALISON MOYET I think people probably perceive me in that way. I do tend to be excessive in most of the things that I do, yes. I've got a very addictive nature and I like to do things to a point which is almost damaging.

INTERVIEWER What sort of things do you like to get addicted to?

ALISON MOYET Anything that's addictive.

INTERVIEWER Anything?

ALISON MOYET Well, for example, I don't like the taste of alcohol. I only drink to get drunk. So if I drink I'll drink to fall over. I won't drink because I enjoy the taste of it. If I have sex, it's a destructive thing. I don't do it to make love . . . particularly.

INTERVIEWER Have you ever tried drugs?

ALISON MOYET Yeah.

INTERVIEWER Are you worried about getting addicted to them?

ALISON MOYET No, because I had a really bad part of my
   life where I really thought it would be quite wonderful
   to take something horribly toxic and end in a lovely cloud
   of smoke. But I'm a single parent and I've got two kids
   and I've got to look after them, so there's that part of me
   that will never allow it, you know? I don't shirk my
   responsibilities. When I decide to get drunk to the point
   of vomiting it's at a weekend when one of the fathers has
   the children.

   This extract underlines the way in which an addictive
lifestyle has become an accepted norm in society. It may
represent the extreme end of the spectrum of dependency
but it still shows how societies like ours have become pro-
foundly addictive in character. Indeed, my argument in this
book is that we have taken on many of the characteristics
anticipated by Aldous Huxley in *Brave New World*. We have
become a society 'high' on *soma*, sex, the feelies, Solidarity
Services, and many other things besides. In the process, we
have all of us, to quote the hymn 'Lord, for the years'
by Timothy Dudley-Smith, become 'oppressed by pleasure,
wealth and care'.
   I want to argue that in this situation the Church has the
unique responsibility of providing an alternative community
of resistance and liberation. Indeed, the major task ahead of
us in the nineties is to establish a brave new Church which
can function as a radical counter-culture within a nation
strongly under the influence of hedonism. It is my purpose
in this final chapter to sketch some of the priorities for such
a Church.

A call to repentance

The phrase 'brave new Church' implies that the Church as it is right now is far from effective in the world. That is certainly the case, as the statistics (at least as far as churchgoing is concerned) amply demonstrate. The truth of the matter is that people in our addictive society are not queueing up at churches to find salvation. As Aldous Huxley remarked in *The Doors of Perception*,

> Countless persons desire self-transcendence and would be glad to find it in church. But alas, 'the hungry sheep look up and are not fed'. They take part in rites, they listen to sermons, they repeat prayers; but their thirst remains unassuaged.[2]

The result is, says Huxley, people reject church and choose an addiction instead. 'Disappointed, they turn to the bottle.' As Huxley puts it:

> When, for whatever reason, men and women fail to transcend themselves by means of worship, good works and spiritual exercises, they are apt to resort to religion's chemical surrogates.[3]

The problem is that the Churches in Britain have not offered the unchurched population what they really need. We have not provided them with a sense of the powerful reality of God in worship. We have not offered the Good News of the Cross in a way that scratches where our generation has been itching. We have not offered people a vibrant, caring, outer-directed community in which addictive behaviour can be lovingly addressed. What we have offered instead is what Huxley describes as

> the mild sense of virtue which sustains the average

Sunday churchgoer through ninety minutes of
boredom.[4]

There is therefore a great need to get on our knees and
repent, to turn back to God, so that our sins may be
wiped out, and times of refreshing may come from the
Lord (Acts 3:19). Before renewal can occur there must be
a season of repentance. Lamenting over the sins of our
Church (whatever the denomination) is the necessary
prelude to the revival that both the Church and the world
so desperately need.

The addicted Church

One of the most obvious reasons why the Church has
not made a noticeable impact on an addictive society is
that the Church itself shows evidence of addiction. There
is evidence in our Christian lives of many of the different
kinds of addiction identified in Chapter 4. Many leaders
and their congregations suffer from ingestive, process,
people, ideological and technological addictions. Many
clergy suffer, in particular, from work addiction.

Addiction to work is widespread amongst Church professionals today.[5] One reason for this is that it is easy to
believe that selfless busyness is consistent with the Gospel.
Many of us do not think of excessive work for God as
harmful. Alcohol is clearly addictive; hard work for the
Lord is less clearly so. After all, did not Paul say, 'I have
worked harder than all of the apostles' (1 Cor. 15:10)?
Does not our Protestant work ethic encourage us to live
a life of constant industry? No wonder many clergy preach
'justification by faith' but end up living 'justification by
busyness'. The situation is not helped when people in the

Church praise and respect such ministers for their full
diaries and their astonishing work rate. Hearing others
say 'I don't know how you do it' is received as a compli-
ment; flattery then fuels the addiction.

But workaholism is not the only addiction within the
Church. Sexual addiction is another area of concern; and
hardly a month goes by without some story being published in the tabloid press on this subject. Sexual addiction
is particularly common in the Church because of a
number of factors:[6]

1. Church authority has traditionally been invoked to
   condemn sexual behaviour. This provides the essential
   ingredient to psychological obsession: the forbidden.
   The fusion of the erotic with the forbidden creates the
   perfect environment for obsessive behaviour.
2. In many circles Church leaders are increasingly larger-
   than-life figures, often appearing in the media, frequently on platforms at major conferences. Putting
   ministers on pedestals in this way can make them very
   vulnerable to those who are attracted by figures with
   status.
3. Male clergy often spend a good deal of time on their
   own with women from their churches. Though many
   Christians now advise that men counsel men and
   women counsel women, there are still situations in
   any church in which a trusted minister could enter a
   dependency relationship with a member of the
   opposite sex.
4. Selfless, unceasing service to the needs of others can
   lead to intense emotional poverty on the part of the
   minister. Personal needs may be left unmet as a result
   of a martyr-like work ethic. Personal depletion through
   severe overwork can lead to sexual addiction.

Other addictions lie just beneath the surface of Church life. James Royce, writing of the Roman Catholic Church in the USA, argues that many clergy are alcohol addicts. When alcohol and prescription drugs are simply an accepted part of society, this, Royce contends, is inevitable:

> Wine at dinner is no longer only for big feasts in the convent, and beer is presumed to be a harmless source of conviviality. Neither is recognized as having the same alcohol as hard liquor, and as having the danger of addiction. Alcohol in some form is considered a necessity for any picnic or social gathering, male or female. Our good Catholic doctors prescribe tranquillizers and sleeping pills on the naive presumption that no sister or priest could possibly be a 'junkie' or addict.[7]

No wonder then that:

> The percentage of alcoholism and other addictions among priests and religious is now being reported as probably higher than in the average population.[8]

Another addiction that has recently been identified as rife in the Church (particularly in North America) is 'religious addiction'. In his book *Regaining Control* (subtitled *When Good Things Become Addictions*), Grant Martin defines this particular addiction as follows:

> Addiction to religion occurs when the focus is taken off of God, and emotional priority is given to people or programmes. The spiritual addict then uses religious ritual and emotional manipulation as the object or experience to produce a change in mood.[9]

The religious addict is someone whose primary goal is to

obtain some form of mood-altering, emotional encounter in and through religion. Because the setting of this particular form of addiction is a pious one (as opposed to a bar, a brothel, or a betting office, for example), the addict easily justifies the dependency. Like the religious workaholic, the religious addict legitimises what is ultimately excessive and destructive behaviour.

Ideological addictions

In Chapter 4 I identified five categories of addiction: ingestive, process, relational, technological, and ideological addictions. This last category – which I defined as the attachment to certain 'isms' – is particularly visible in Churches today. Here are a few examples of the 'isms' upon which we can become dependent.

Individualism

This is one of the primary idols of our age. It manifests itself in church life when people start to believe that their own needs are of far greater importance than the Christian community to which they belong. Thus, for example, the individualist says, 'I'll go to the home group that I want to go to', rather than, 'I'll go to the home group where I will have most to offer'.

Privatism

Some people in the Church have a rather developed form of individualism known as privatism. Privatists believe that faith is a personal option, not a public value; as a result, they keep their religion entirely to themselves. Faith is entirely a private matter. The privatist or secularist would no sooner talk about his or her religious views than about any other very personal matter. Faith sharing is therefore never practised.

Romanticism

This is the worship of past traditions. Many churchgoers are highly resistant to change of any kind. 'It has always been done this way', is their rallying cry. The problem is that this is more than just a nostalgia for former things; behind many such comments there is an actual attachment to former traditions. This dependency needs to be recognised like any other.

Materialism

This is another primary idol. It is manifested in Church life in many ways: in the extraordinary amounts of Church money that are invested in shopping malls and other commercial ventures; in the prosperity gospel, which argues that health and wealth can be claimed by every believer through the power of positive confession; in the reluctance of many churchgoers to give generously to their local churches.

Hedonism

Hedonism is the pursuit of pleasure and happiness for one's own sake. There is plenty of this amongst Christians today. Many churchgoers have simply added Christianity as a means of comfort to an already comfortable lifestyle. Not for them a radical discipleship of simplicity and of dying to self: what matters is the extra pleasure and comfort gained from going to church and being seen to be going to church.

Institutionalism

Institutionalism is manifested in anyone who worships the Church rather than the Lord. In the historic Churches there are plenty of people who are more in love with the institution than they are with the Lord Jesus Christ. They love the pomp, the ceremony, the prestige, the status, and the traditionalism of their denomination. They cannot stop talking about such things. As Bishop Michael Marshall said at a recent conference, 'God hates the church most when it speaks about itself. But he loves it most when it speaks about his Son.'

Clericalism

There is still evidence in many clergy (and also those seeking ordination) of an addiction to holy orders. The power and the position that the office of priest is deemed to confer on people can become the object of excessive dependency and attachment. Furthermore, for some clergy the actual position itself can become a source of obsession. All that matters is their priestly office. An addiction to authority and control often forms part of this matrix of obsessive behaviour.

Legalism

Many churches – particularly in the conservative evangelical constituency – are in a state of denial about their level of addictiveness to law. In such churches there are rules to be obeyed if one is to be considered 'sound'. A particular jargon must be adopted if one is to be considered an insider. Here the problem is what one American GP, in relation to the drug Prozac, calls 'musturbation': the tyranny of 'I must' and 'I ought' holds sway. Grace is preached, but law is practised.

Consumerism

As many realise, shopping has become our main national pastime. It used to be said that our philosophy could be summed up in Descartes' words, 'I think, therefore I am': some Christian writers today argue that the dictum needs changing to 'I shop, therefore I am'. This consumerist philosophy has affected religion. The relationship between shopping and religion is a complex one: shopping has become a religious experience, and religion has become for many a consumerist product – in other words, a matter of shopping around for the church (or churches) of one's choice. Many Christians, faced with the choice between going to a local centre of worship which might cost us more, and the more distant megachurch that seems to offer us everything we need, will choose the latter . . . not realising that they have adopted the addictive values of a consumerist society.

These are just some of the ideological addictions or 'isms' present in the Church today. There are others as well: racism, escapism (avoiding the social pain of the growing underclass and of the third world), egoism (seeking a platform for oneself), sensationalism (church services in which only dramatic demonstrations of spiritual power will do), ageism (writing off the elderly), sexism (particularly the oppression of women), and so on. All of

these may be addictions: they are things upon which we
may, as Christians, become dependent.

The Church as an addicted system

One of the main reasons why the Church has not had
greater impact on society is therefore that it has confor-
med to the pattern of this world rather than transformed
the world by the renewal of its mind (Rom. 12:2). It has
become an addicted Church. Anne Wilson Schaef's book,
When Society Becomes an Addict, is particularly helpful in
defining at this point what we mean by 'an addicted
Church'. One of her central arguments is that institutions
in the West take on the characteristics of an addict. Larger
social systems – such as schools, churches and govern-
ments – behave as individual addicts do. Below are some
of the things that the individual addict and an addicted
social system have in common.[10]

Self-centredness

Addicts are self-centred people whose fix overshadows
everything else. 'The alcoholic thinks only of the next
drink, the relationship addict of the next affair, the workaholic of the next item on the agenda'.[11] Schaef proposes
that social systems function in exactly this way. They
too can become self-orientated and narcissistic; they can
become self-centred rather than outer-directed.

The illusion of control

The addict thinks she is in control of her addiction,
whereas the reverse is in fact the truth: her addiction con-

trols her. In an addicted social system, Schaef proposes
that control is a real issue. 'The family tries to control the
addict, the addict tries to control the family, the spouse
tries to control against being controlled; everyone is
involved in some kind of addictive behaviour'.[12]

Dishonesty

'Practicing drunks', says Schaef, 'are consummate liars.
They lie about how much, when, where, with whom,
and whether. Frequent and habitual lying is one of the
more evident signs of alcohol or drug abuse'.[13] Like
the drunk, a social system or an institution can become
dishonest.

Confusion

The life of the addict is a life in which confusion is the
norm. So long as confusion is present, the addict is powerless to deal with his addiction. In addicted systems, much
time and energy are spent trying to figure out what is
really going on. Leaders of institutions use veiled language
and are 'economical with the truth'. This leads to a sense
of powerlessness and confusion lower down in the system.

Denial

Denial is perhaps the classic symptom of the addict. 'Problem? What problem? I could give up any time.' 'Denial',
Schaef writes, 'is the addict's major defense mechanism.'[14]
Social systems can also betray this trait. If an institution
maintains a façade of respectability and stability when
there really are serious problems, then that institution is
manifesting denial.

Perfectionism

'Alcoholics, drug addicts, compulsive overeaters are perfectionists', says Schaef. 'They are convinced that nothing they do is ever good enough, that *they* are never good enough'.[15] Social systems can get into perfectionism as soon as they become addicted. Mistakes, in such institutions, are unacceptable: if mistakes are made, they must be covered up.

Forgetfulness

The addict is amongst the most forgetful of people. He loses his keys, forgets to pick up the children, misses meetings, and so on. The addicted social system is similarly forgetful. It does not place importance on the past, because the present system is the only thing that matters.

Scarcity

The addict is selfish in the extreme. She hoards money, material goods, love, and prestige. She does this on the grounds that there is not enough to go round (the scarcity model). The addicted system operates in a similar way. Schaef writes that 'The addictive system must continually have more bombs, a larger gross national product, more money, more influence. No matter what we do as a nation and as a society, it is never enough'.[16]

Negativism

The addict perceives himself, others and the world in negative terms. The addicted system likewise promotes negative thinking: it is critical and judgmental, rather than supportive or positive.

Defensiveness

The addict cannot accept feedback or criticism. She is a defensive, insecure person. Similarly, the addicted system has its defensive aspects; it is always concerned about promoting how right it is.

Frozen feelings

Addicts are almost totally out of touch with their feelings. Addictions succeed in suppressing anger, fear, joy and so on. In the addicted system too, people are not allowed to express or show their feelings: in such societies and institutions, feelings become frozen.

This list of the chief characteristics of an addicted social system is helpful in assessing the extent to which our own Church has become addicted in character. Ask yourself the following questions about your own Church, looking at the local, the national and the international levels:

1. Is it outer-directed or inward-looking?
2. Is there evidence of control in your Church?
3. Does your Church encourage honesty and vulner-
   ability?
4. Is there confusion?
5. Does it maintain a façade of respectability and
   stability when in truth things are far from right?
6. Is it a place where mistakes are allowed?
7. Does your Church have a healthy sense of history?

8. Is scarcity (never having enough resources) a problem?
9. Does your Church perceive outsiders in negative terms?
10. Is it judgmental and critical?
11. Are open demonstrations of joy, sorrow, and anger allowed?

Perhaps you are experiencing at this point what Alcoholics Anonymous call 'an awakening', for it is hard to ignore the realisation that we *are* an addicted Church in an addictive society. No wonder we have made so little impact in recent decades. No wonder the statistics for churchgoing in Great Britain are so disturbingly low. There is clearly a need for repentance before anything else. The Lord must be permitted to come and cleanse his temple.

Not like the Gentiles

As an aid to this process of repentance we need to be guided by the Scriptures. I have found Paul's Letter to the Ephesians particularly relevant in this respect. Indeed, much of Ephesians seems to me to be especially prophetic in an addictive society. It seems that the Christians in Ephesus were finding it difficult resisting the pleasures on offer in their fair city, and some were starting to forget what they had learnt during their baptismal instruction and were falling back into old ways. In this situation of degeneracy, Paul – I do take the author to be Paul – offers an example of what, in addictionology, is termed 'tough love':

So I tell you this, and insist on it in the Lord, that

> you must no longer live as the Gentiles do, in the
> futility of their thinking. They are darkened in their
> understanding and separated from the life of God
> because of the ignorance that is in them due to the
> hardening of their hearts. Having lost all sensitivity,
> they have given themselves over to sensuality so as
> to indulge in every kind of impurity, with a contin-
> ual lust for more. (Eph. 4:17–19)

Paul here speaks assertively to his congregation in Ephesus. The believers there are, he insists, to resist the pagan,
Gentile mindset which is utterly futile. Theirs is to be an
attitude of confrontation rather than accommodation. He
then spells out eight qualities of this mindset, which have
a remarkable similarity to aspects of addiction.

The first thing Paul says about the thinking of Gentiles
is that they are 'darkened in their understanding'. Here we
may trace parallels with what Schaef calls 'the abnormal
thinking processes' of addicts. Addicts, in truth, are
amongst the most irrational of people. The following
example bears this out:

> Consider three priests in a treatment programme
> for sexual addiction. Each offered their rationale for
> preserving their celibacy. One thought of himself as
> an 'emotional virgin' since he had only been sexual
> with prostitutes with whom he had had no relation-
> ship. Another explained that his celibacy was intact
> because he was sexual with men and not women.
> The third had only been sexual with people in his
> own order and so perceived his vow of celibacy as
> not violated.[17]

This is certainly irrational thinking or darkened understanding. It reveals the very subtle ways in which the mind

of the addict seeks to justify and rationalise destructive behaviour.

The second thing Paul says about the Gentile mindset is that it is 'separated from the life of God'. Here again there are parallels with addiction. Recently, experts have been suggesting that addiction is a disease with serious spiritual consequences. In their own way they have been suggesting that an excessive attachment to anything can 'separate a person from the life of God'. Some remarks by James Royce are relevant at this point:

> Alcohol and other drugs impair one's ability to think and feel right about God, to function in relation to God as one should. The result is spiritual dis-ease. One cannot be comfortable in the presence of the Creator, gets distorted ideas of God or feelings towards God which make it difficult to really trust and love. One is ill-at-ease with God, not attuned to the Infinite . . .[18]

Thirdly, Paul uses the word 'ignorance'. I equate ignorance with the classic symptom of denial. The addict lacks honest self-knowledge: he thinks he is in control, when in reality his life has become unmanageable. The addict says, 'I am not an alcoholic. I could give up drinking tomorrow.' The addict therefore lacks true knowledge: he is ignorant.

Fourthly, Paul says of Gentiles that they have undergone 'hardening of their hearts'. Paul means that pagans have a stubborn resistance to the life and the truth of God, right at the very core of their beings. They are so steeped in their addicted lifestyles that they aggressively resist offers of salvation. The same goes for addicts, as the family members and friends of an addict could testify. Opportunities to achieve recovery through a Twelve-Step programme are often resisted with resentment and hostility. The heart of an addict is truly hard. As Schaef writes, 'Addicts are notoriously self-centred. They may claim to care about the people around them, but their fix begins to overshadow everything else'.[19]

The fifth thing Paul says about the Gentile mindset is that it has 'lost all sensitivity'. Here the Greek word is *apolgekotes*. This is the only instance of it in the New Testament, and refers to the anaesthetising of one's moral and spiritual sense. Here again there are striking parallels with addiction. Royce says,

> Alcohol or marijuana or pills anaesthetize one's sensitivity to spiritual values. Religion becomes sick: mechanical, shallow, external, instead of deeply felt and experienced. Spiritual life becomes dormant, but one is anaesthetized to that fact, too.[20]

Truly, the addict is *apolgekotes* – insensate.

Sixthly, Paul says of Gentiles that they have 'given themselves over to sensuality'. Here again there are obvious parallels with the addicted mindset. 'Given over' is better translated 'handed over' (*paredokan* in Greek). This links the process nicely with addiction. As I remarked in Chapter 4, the word 'addiction' comes from the Latin verb *addicere* meaning to 'hand over', or 'surrender'. An addict is someone who has handed her life over to be controlled by her addiction. In Ephesians 4.19, Paul uses the word 'sensuality' as the thing to which the Gentile surrenders his life. Sensuality is indulgence in anything pleasurable to the senses. That is precisely what addictions offer: mood-altering holidays from reality, which bring temporary – all too temporary – sensual pleasure.

Seventhly, Paul says that Gentiles 'indulge in every kind of impurity'. The Greek word translated 'impurity' is *akatharsia,* which connotes excessive and riotous behaviour, especially sexual behaviour. This also has parallels with addiction. Though few addictions actually involve riotous behaviour, all addictions can be summed up as 'behaviour in excess', and, as we saw in Chapter 3, erotic behaviour is a particularly common expression of that in our culture right now.

Finally, Paul says that the Gentiles way of life involves 'a continual lust [or craving] for more'. Here the word is *pleonexia,* which refers to a greed that can never be satisfied. What is it that addicts suffer from but *pleonexia?* The person on soft drugs needs after a while to take harder drugs. In order to sustain the 'high', the addict has to move on to harder drugs, harder pornography, harder liquor, and so on. The addict truly has a continual craving for more.

The problem of idolatry

In Ephesians 4:17–19 Paul has captured with wonderful astuteness some of the chief characteristics of addiction. To Christians in Ephesus he says, 'I insist that you resolutely avoid living the addictive and destructive lifestyle of the pagans around you.' In the words that follow in Ephesians 4–5, Paul goes on to describe some of the specific addictions which have evidently become visible in the Church:

- speaking lies about others (4:25);
- expressing anger (4:26);
- stealing (4:28);
- unwholesome talk (4:29);
- bitterness (4:31);

- brawling (4:31);
- slander (4:31)
- malice (4:31);
- sexual immorality (5:3);
- impurity (5:3);
- greed (5:3);
- obscenity (5:4);
- foolish talk or coarse joking (5:4).

In Ephesians 5.5, Paul then goes on to describe the reason why all such things must be staunchly resisted:

> For of this you can be sure: No immoral, impure or greedy person – such a man is an idolater – has any inheritance in the Kingdom of Christ and of God.

The key word in this tough warning is the word 'idolater', for there is a connection between idolatry and addiction. An addiction is an excessive attachment to a substance, a pattern of behaviour, a person, a value system, or an object: it is the state of being dependent on something or someone. This, in short, is idolatry. It is turning something or someone other than God into an object of worship. All addictions are therefore idolatrous, because they eclipse God.

Herein lies the real need for repentance. Our addictions are not just sicknesses, they are idolatries. Aldous Huxley came to recognise this in the latter stages of his life. He wrote a good deal about idolatry in some of his later, religious essays. In 'Seven meditations' he defines idolatry as follows:

> Idolatry consists in loving a creature more than we love God.[21]

In 'Substitutes for liberation', Huxley describes some of the idols we bow down to:

> Theory has undergone a change, but not practice;
> for in practice millions upon millions of civilized
> men and women continue to pay their devotions,
> not to the liberating spirit, but to alcohol, to hashish,
> to opium and its derivatives, to barbiturates and the
> other synthetic additions to the age-old catalogue of
> poisons capable of causing self-transcendence.[22]

Huxley's view (frequently articulated in his later essays
on religion) was that idols are destructive. He wrote that:

> Every idol, however exalted, turns out in the long
> run to be a Moloch, hungry for human sacrifices.[23]

In his essay on 'Idolatry', he identified what he called
'the moral fault' that lies within the worship of idols. This
consists in

> the setting up of some idea which is most kindred
> to our own minds, and the putting it in the place
> of Christ.[24]

A radical renunciation of idols is therefore what Huxley
advocates. 'God's kingdom cannot come unless we begin
by making our human kingdoms go.'

Sleeping with the enemy

Huxley himself was aware that the word 'idolatry' was
somewhat outmoded, even in his own day. In 'Who are
we?' he explains why the word must be recaptured and
used today:

> I remember as a boy reading in the Ten Command-
> ments the warning against idolatry, and wondering
> why such a fuss should be made about this, because,

after all, who cares whether people take their hats off to a statue or not! But it is much profounder than this. Idolatry is in fact the worship of a part – especially the self or projection of the self – as though it were the absolute totality.[25]

Huxley pointed in his essays to the different examples of idols in his own time: alcohol, drugs, crowd delirium, authority and control, music ('the ecstasy-producing rite of rhythmic sound'), technology, politics, nationalism, Communism, Fascism, and so on. He argued very persuasively that idolatry is not just confined to the world of ancient Israel: it is a widespread problem today.

For a brave new Church to emerge, one imperative is therefore the confrontation and destruction of idols. If the Church is to offer any real alternative in such an addictive, idolatrous culture as ours, then we have to acknowledge that we have been sleeping with the enemy. We have to acknowledge our need of a radical and transformative awakening.

Paul uses the language of awakening in Ephesians 5:14. He reminds his readers that their conversion and baptism in Christ was an awakening. When they were baptised in water and the Holy Spirit, they were woken out of the terminal lethargy of sin into real, resurrection life. That is why the congregation, at the moment when a new convert came out of the waters, sang the hymn cited in Ephesians 5:14:

> Wake up, O sleeper,
> Rise from the dead,
> And Christ will shine upon you!

Paul uses these words to remind the Church in Ephesus

that they must not revert to the addictive way of life they had led before their baptism. During their preparation for baptism, they were scrutinised for evidence of such addictive, idolatrous attachments and were no doubt instructed and prayed out of them. That is why Paul declares in Ephesians 4:21, 'Surely you heard of him and were taught in him in accordance with the truth that is in Jesus'. He reminds them that they were taught to live as 'children of the light' (5:8), not as disobedient people whose deeds are done in secret (5:12; another characteristic of addiction). He exhorts them to have nothing to do with the fruitless deeds of darkness (5:11).

This teaching can be illustrated from the story of the film coincidentally called *Awakenings* (from the book by Oliver Sacks). In the film, Robin Williams plays the part of a doctor who is sent to a hospital full of people suffering from a very rare and perplexing disease. It is called *encephalitis lethargica*, and is an illness that reduces people to a seemingly permanent state of sleep. As the plot unfolds, the doctor appears to find a cure, and the patients start to enjoy a life they had been denied for years. The world is alerted to the extraordinary recoveries of the patients in the hospital. Sadly, however, these awakenings fail to last and, to the doctor's deep grief, the patients slip back into the 'lethargica' from which he had, for a brief time, awoken them.

Going back to Ephesians, Paul writes that we, before we came to know Christ, were like people asleep – suffering from a spiritual 'lethargica' or numbness. However, with our conversion and baptism, Christ himself shone a light into our lives and woke us up from our moral and spiritual sleep. Christ was, as it were, the doctor who brought us our 'awakening'. Paul warns us not to revert to the former state of darkness. Reverting to a sinful, addicted lifestyle is as senseless as choosing to re-enter a state of *encephalitis lethargica*. The problem is, of course, that many of us in the Church today have not heeded Paul's warning. We need to acknowledge that we have offended against God's holy law by allowing his Church to become so addicted and so idolatrous. The call to the Church is therefore one of repentance.

Twelve steps to wholeness

As an aid to that repentence, we may find some help from the following, Christianised version of the Twelve-Step programme.

STEP 1 *We admit we are powerless over our addictions – that our lives have become unmanageable*
The admission of powerlessness is absolutely essential if repentance is to occur. Sooner or later we come to a crisis and recognise that we are over-attached to things or people, and that these attachments are sin. The first step is to admit with Paul, 'What I do is not the good I want to do; no, the evil I do not want to do – this I keep doing' (Rom. 7:19).

STEP 2 *We confess that the Holy Spirit, a power much greater than ourselves, can restore us to wholeness*
If Step 1 is about admitting our powerlessness, Step 2 is about believing in God's power to save us. AA groups talk often about a 'higher power' which can restore addicts to wholeness. The individual is left to decide what that higher power really is. For Christians, the power which saves us from the terminal spiral of addiction is the power of the Holy Spirit.

God, praying for more love and more power to live a holy and healed life
Step 11 encourages us to increase our intimacy with God through devotional prayer and through practising the healing presence of God.

STEP 12 *Having had a spiritual awakening as the result of these steps, we try to carry this message to others*
Step 12 places an emphasis on gratitude for God's grace. It also places great emphasis upon telling others of the salvation and healing we have found in Jesus. It stresses the importance of looking outwards to the unsaved, addictive culture rather than inwards to ourselves. It stresses power evangelism, not power fellowship.

Using a programme like this with a trusted friend, in a home group, in a church meeting, or even at a national Church congress, might well help to detoxify the Church from its addictions.

A great awakening

A season of repentance is therefore needed, and repentance – as we all know – is a radical and ruthless turning from sin. It is not just saying sorry.

This season of repentance, if genuine, would not last forever; if it did, we would simply have succeeded in transforming one form of self-absorption into another, and the world outside the Church would still be unhealed, unsaved and untouched. Sooner or later there will be a turning of our hearts from a penitential introspection to a new passion for a true expression of the kingdom of God in the world. Lamentation will then be formed into intercession. The deep emotions of grief concerning the state of the Church will be turned into an equally deep emotion of grief concerning the state of the world. Having had our own sins, addictions and idols so clearly set before us, we will see the world with all its lost souls, and our hearts will compel us to pray for revival in the Church and in society at large. In other words, having had our own awakening, we will pray for a great awakening, an awakening of the world to its sinfulness, to its utter need for its Creator God, and to the wonderful saving mercy of Jesus revealed in the Calvary event.

What kind of things does our 'brave new Church' need to be working on in order to prepare for such a widespread movement of the Holy Spirit? Most of our Church life can be reduced to three things: mission, community, and worship. Below I suggest some ways in which we could develop these three foundations of our ecclesial life in ways that might benefit society at large.

Mission

Our society needs the Gospel. There are countless people who are crying out in pain and who, confronted by the hole in the soul, are finding false and destructive ways of anaesthetising themselves. Witness the following words, written by an unknown drug addict:[26]

> King heroin is my shepherd, I shall always want,
> He maketh me to lie down in the gutters.
> He leadeth me beside the troubled waters.
> He destroyeth my soul.
> He leadeth me in the paths of wickedness for
>   the effort's sake.
> Yea, I shall walk through the valley of poverty

and fear all evil, for thou, heroin, art with me;
thy needle and capsule try to comfort me;
Thou strippest the table of groceries in the
presence of my family; thou robbest my head of
reason, my cup of sorrow runneth over.
Surely, heroin addiction shall stalk me all the
days of my life, and I will dwell in the house of
the damned forever.

Those words were found by a policeman on a card in a telephone booth. On the reverse side, the addict had written this postscript:

Truly this is my psalm. I am a young woman, 20 years of age and for the past year and a half have been wandering down the nightmare alley of the junkie. I want to quit taking dope and I try but I can't. Prison didn't help me, nor did the hospital for long. The doctor told my family it would have been better and indeed kinder if the person who first got me hooked on dope would have taken a gun and blown my brains out and I wish to God she had! How I wish she had!

In the light of this sad tale we have to confess that there is something wrong with the Church's witness to the nation. If a young woman of 20 can resort to a drug like heroin rather than to spiritual salvation, then there is something badly amiss with the Church's presentation of Jesus to the world. Something is wrong somewhere. Part of the problem, I believe, concerns the Church's lack of confidence about the uniqueness of Jesus Christ. Jesus said, 'I am the way, the truth, and the life' (John 14:6). To this claim our society says a resounding 'No!' The pluralist says, 'There are many ways to God, not just one

single way. Jesus was wrong. He is *a* way, not *the* way.'
The relativist says, 'There are many truths about God.
There is no one, ultimate, absolute truth. Jesus was wrong.
He is *a* truth. He is not *the* truth.' The hedonist says,
'There are many ways of enjoying life today. I do not
deny that some people may find a better life through
Christianity. But Christianity is *a* life. It is not *the* life.' In
other words, our culture is one that has become pro-
foundly resistant to exclusivity in religious claims – such
claims are now deemed politically and religiously
incorrect.

In a culture saturated with the ideological values of
pluralism, relativism and hedonism, the Church has lost
confidence in its Christology – in its understanding of
the nature and significance of Jesus Christ. Going back
to Paul's letter to the Ephesians, however, we should note
that within only a few decades of Jesus' death, Paul was
talking of Jesus in highly exalted terms. These are a few
examples from Chapter 1 alone:

- our Lord Jesus Christ (1:3);
- the One he loves (1:6);
- in him we have redemption (1:7);
- one head, even Christ (1:10);
- Christ, raised from the dead (1:20);
- seated at God's right hand (1:20).

Paul ends that sequence with an open, bold and unequivo-
cal statement of the ultimacy of Christ. He writes that
Jesus Christ is:

> Far above all rule, authority, power and dominion,
> and every title that can be given, not only in the
> present age, but also in the one to come. And God
> placed all things under his feet and appointed him

to be head over everything for the church, which is
his body, the fulness of him who fills everything in
every way. (Eph. 1:21–3)

Here, in a culture every bit as addictive as ours, Paul
confidently proclaims the highest possible Christology.
That is an important reminder. The Church that will
make inroads in the uncertain, pluralistic situation in
which we find ourselves today will surely be a Church
that finds meaningful ways of talking about Jesus to an
addictive society. This means preaching a Jesus who
walked where we walk and who felt what we feel. It
means talking about a Jesus who went to the Cross for
our sins, who died the most excruciating death so that
we might be forgiven. It means proclaiming a Jesus who
said, to use the words of AA, 'no pain, no gain' – a Jesus
who refused an anaesthetic at Calvary precisely because
he knew that the experience of pain had to be taken back
to the Godhead as a gift. On that issue there must be no
compromise. Martin Scorsese's version of the crucifixion
in the film *The Last Temptation of Christ* (in which Jesus
has a sexual fantasy on the Cross) is offensive not so much
because it clearly disobeys Jesus' own teaching in Matthew
5:28, as because it highlights our society's inability to face
any pain without resorting to addictive behaviour. But
that was not Jesus' way. Jesus embraced the pain, and there
is something truly paradigmatic about that for a culture
where the removal of pain is one of the highest priorities.

We need to learn to talk about Jesus in a way that is
appropriate for an addictive society, and to talk about him
freely and confidently. For example, one area in which
Christology could be fruitfully developed is around the
concept of Jesus as our liberator, as the one who sets us
free from our sins, from our wounds, and from our addic-

tions. Latin American liberation theologians often use
this concept in their struggle against the oppression of
punishment and injustice. (The El Salvadorian scholar Jon
Sobrino is a fine example.) But we face oppression too –
the oppression of what Huxley called 'the new totalitarianism'. We need liberation, albeit from the oppression
of pleasure rather than of pain. The historical Jesus, at the
start of his ministry, announced:

> The Spirit of the Lord is on me,
>   because he has anointed me
>   to preach good news to the poor.
> He has sent me to proclaim freedom for the prisoners,
>   and recovery of sight to the blind,
>   to release the oppressed,
>   to proclaim the year of the Lord's favour.
>   (Luke 4:18–19)

From these words we can see that the real Jesus saw
himself as the Spirit-anointed liberator of Isaiah 61:1–2.
That being so, I would argue that this truth has a profound
relevance in our addictive society. Indeed, even the language of the Isaianic quotation seems tailor-made for
us, with its talk of freedom, oppression, and particularly
'recovery'. In this text, at least, we may find some
resources for evangelising an addictive society.

What I am suggesting, therefore, is a regained confidence in the uniqueness of Jesus Christ, and a concomi-
tant search for new ways of communicating this
uniqueness in a hedonistic culture. As another example,
let me indicate one very simple word which may be of
some help. I was reminded of this word when reading a
recent report about the tragic death of a woman named
Alethea:

Over and over again Lady Alethea Savile had tried
to cure herself of her addiction to crack. But the
depression that the drug temporarily alleviated won
yet again on that September evening. She had sought
treatment five times in an attempt to conquer her
melancholy and her addiction to drugs and alcohol.
But each time she was unable to resist going back.

She knew the ritual, of course: fill the glass pipe
with water, place the lump of crack . . . on tinfoil,
perforated with a matchstick the better to inhale the
fumes. As always, the high lasted only a few minutes.
Desperate to maintain it, Alethea finished her entire
stash, chain-smoking Silk Cut and gulping down
sedatives to calm her nerves as she 'came down'.
Then she went into her bedroom and collapsed into
a coma. She was only 31.[27]

It seemed to me, reading this story, that there was a
strange, almost tragic irony in the name of this woman,
for 'Aletheia' comes from the Greek word *aletheia*, meaning 'reality' or 'truth'. How poignant, then, that the one
thing that Alethea could not face was 'reality'. But reading
the report my mind also turned to John's gospel, for
there the word *aletheia* occurs 25 times. In fact, nearly
half the uses of *aletheia* in the New Testament can be
found in John, and in 1, 2, and 3 John. When Jesus says,
'I am the truth' in John 14:6, the word translated 'truth'
is *aletheia*. When Pilate, looking (ironically) at Jesus asks,
'What is truth?' the word again is *aletheia*. Surely here, in
a society in which people are trying to find liberation
through virtual reality, we have a rich resource for a
meaningful Christology in the modern world – Jesus, our
ultimate reality.

Community

A brave new Church will be a Church with a confident
and pertinent Christology. It will also be a Church with
a sense of true community, for one of the things that is
most lacking in our culture at present is just such a sense of
community. I remember giving a lecture on our addictive
society at a theological college a few years ago. A South
African pastor said to me afterwards:

> I don't think it's possible for people in this country
> to live without some kind of addiction. In my
> country, at least if someone falls, if someone is hurt,
> if someone suffers, there is a nexus of relationships
> which, like a net, can catch and sustain them. In
> your country, there are no such networks. People
> have to look elsewhere for support and sustenance.

That is a fair and perceptive remark. Our society offers
so many temporary, momentary communities – commut-
ing together, a shared ride in a theme park, sitting in the
same fast-food restaurant, shopping together in malls. In
this vacuum, new models of community need to be discovered and established. Howard Rheingold, in his
impressive book *The Virtual Community: Finding Connection in a Computerised World*,[28] has suggested that the Net
is the answer. Using the Net, you can access any virtual
friend in the world. You can find support for crises you are
experiencing IRL ('in real life') by contacting a particular
support group via your modem. The problem with this
view, as Rheingold does actually concede, is that virtual
community can end up being no kind of community at
all. In the final analysis, it may just be another fix for
those who are addicted to communication. It may be an
unhealthy outlet for those who desire a level of control

and mastery that they do not have 'IRL'. It is certainly not face-to-face, personal interaction with others.

Virtual community, I would argue, is not true community any more than virtual reality is – if you will forgive the tautology – true reality. True community is a place where, to cite Ephesians 4:15, people can face one another with honesty, and 'speak the truth in love'. True community is what Alcoholics Anonymous call a 'recovery family' – a place where there are no masks, no malice, no deceit, no games, no pretence (Eph. 4:31). True community is somewhere where there is the freedom to be vulnerable and the freedom to own up to our addictions. True community is a place of reality. As David Watson once put it:

> The breakthrough to genuine fellowship comes when Christians stop relating to one another as righteous saints, and start accepting one another as unrighteous sinners. A pious fellowship has no place for the sinner. In such an unreal and super-spiritual atmosphere everyone must wear a mask. We dare not be different. If the true facts about any one of us were exposed the shock would destroy the system; so sin remains trapped in concealed hypocrisy. It is only when we are free to say honestly who and what we are that we discover our true freedom as children of God.[29]

In our own situation we need to take these words about freedom to heart. The world is no longer impressed by the kind of pseudo-pious congregations we have offered in the past. What is needed now is what the liberation theologians call 'basic Christian communities' (BCCs), in which everyone is committed to an honest and radical kingdom lifestyle. These BCCs need to be communities committed to liberation from all forms of cultural addiction. This means that new Christians would undergo a thorough catechesis or baptism preparation which included what used to be called 'the scrutinies'. In a nineties form, this would involve a simple description of addiction, and a process of healing for those enslaved by addictions. It also means fellowship groups being committed to the lifestyle issues of the Sermon on the Mount, which has extremely insightful things to say about addiction (see Appendix 1). In first-world BCCs there has to be an ongoing resistance to the oppression of an addictive society in every aspect of the community's life, from the discipling of new converts, to the sustaining of old ones.

What is therefore needed is authentic community life, in which a low-level ascetism of a joyful kind is being lived out in practical, daily life. Above all, communities committed to facing pain are required – communities where personal pain is dealt with through proper counselling in the power of the Holy Spirit; communities where social and environmental pain are confronted, not denied, and especially issues of poverty and justice; communities, finally, where global pain is felt and addressed. This last point is important. In *Brave New World*, poverty was confined to faraway reservations in Mexico. In the Church there can be no brushing aside of the suffering of the world. Huxley's vision of remote reservations for the poor cannot be a feature of a truly brave new Church.

Worship

What, finally, of the worship in this brave new Church? What we must understand from the start is that addiction is a misuse of the will-to-worship our Creator placed in each one of us. When a person turns to alcohol and becomes excessively attached to it, that person has started to worship something other than God – in this case, drink. The particular appeal of alcohol is, of course, that it can produce effects in us that are not dissimilar from the intense experiences associated with spiritual or mystical ecstasy. Going back to Ephesians, I therefore find it intriguing that Paul offers the following advice about worship to his church there:

> Do not get drunk on wine, which leads to debauchery. Instead, be filled with the Spirit. Speak to one another with psalms, hymns and spiritual songs. Sing and make music in your heart to the Lord, always giving thanks to God the Father for everything, in the name of our Lord Jesus Christ. (Eph. 5:18–20)

What Paul is presenting is a bold antithesis, a stark choice. Either you worship alcohol and get high on its temporary ecstasies, or you worship the Triune God, and experience the elation that comes through encountering the immanent presence and power of the transcendent Lord. Either you fill yourself with an alcoholic spirit, which leads to a terminal life of excess, or you allow yourself to be continuously filled with the Holy Spirit, which leads to a true expression of worship – *speaking* to one another (interestingly) in the words of psalms, hymns and spiritual songs, singing in your heart to the Lord, and living a life of consistent gratitude to the Father.

Herein lies the great choice for our culture today. Whom, or what, are we going to worship? Worshipping anything or anyone other than the Father in heaven is idolatry. Worshipping God in spirit and in truth, on the other hand, is our greatest joy and our ultimate purpose. The problem is, however, that the Church has so often managed to make worship the least relevant, the least meaningful, and the least real thing in an average week. Dr Howard Clinebell makes this point. He argues that a major reason why people become alcoholics is because addiction is a spiritual disease. People, confronted by what Clinebell calls 'existential anxiety', look for pseudo-religious ways of masking that pain, because the Churches fail to offer anything real by way of an encounter with God. As Clinebell says:

> It is pertinent to ask why the alcoholic turns to alcohol in the attempt to handle his existential anxiety. We live in a period of history when it is not easy to find genuinely religious answers. Contemporary religion in the West has lost much of the sense of the numinous and the transcendent . . . Many contemporary religious expressions are pale and anemic, lacking in the ecstatic, the mystical, the numinous. When religion loses its spine-tingling quality, alcohol is substituted by many.[30]

For Christian worship to have any kind of attraction in this particular society a number of adjustments will, I believe, need to be made.

First of all, the preaching must improve. Preachers need to spend more time engaging with popular culture. Sermons then need to be preached with illustrations from this everyday, mainstream culture. They need to be preached with passion, and they need to be preached biblically. In other words, biblical texts that help to illumine and interpret our struggle with an addictive society need to be discovered and shared. What liberation theologians call 'contextualised exegesis' needs to become the norm. Preachers need to carry the Bible in one hand and a newspaper in the other, as 'readers' do in Latin American BCCs. Within this framework, sermons need always to lift up the Lord Jesus Christ, who is the source of our salvation, our wholeness, and our liberation.

Secondly, Christian worship must have a greater visual impact. Go to any seminar in a non-Christian, professional context and the speaker will almost certainly be using state-of-the-art consumer electronics to help make her talk more interesting. Headlines will appear on a smart screen as she discreetly presses the spacebar of a laptop computer. Video sequences and graphic stills will then appear from time to time as the speaker accesses a CD-ROM unit to highlight various points and to retain the audience's attention. Go to a Christian seminar, and what you get instead is an overhead projector. The acetates may be smartly produced – laser-quality print, even colour backgrounds – but it is still just seventies technology. We need to learn from popular culture how to communicate the truths of the Gospel in a visual way, and without falling in love with the technology.

Thirdly, Christian worship must touch our emotions. I do not mean that the Church must start bowing down to the idol of emotionalism: that would make us idolaters of feeling and experience. When that happens, as Huxley wrote,

> the emotion becomes an end in itself, to be eagerly sought after and worshipped, as the addicts of a drug spend life in the pursuit of their artificial paradise.[31]

Those are wise words, and I know a number of charismatic Christian friends who would do well to heed them. However, Christian worship has for far too long been an affair of the head, not of the heart. During this period of the Enlightenment, with its dichotomy of reason and emotion, the Church has too often bought into the culture and opted for a rational rather than a balanced

(reasoned plus emotional) spirituality. I believe it is time
to let the Holy Spirit into our services, to risk experiential
encounters with the Living God, to permit the open
expression of feelings in worship, to play and to celebrate
as well as to pray and to meditate. It is time to give the
control of our worship back to the Lord.

Fourthly, Christian worship needs to incorporate a
sense of history. In other words, it needs to help people
to regain what Hans Georg Gadamer called 'an historical
consciousness'. We are a rootless generation who have lost
a sense of the past. We are a numb generation who have
forgotten that there will be a future. We live in the eternal
present. That, in fact, is one of the characteristics of an
addict. Adrian Van Kaam describes the 'high' of addiction
in this way:

> I live, as it were, in an eternal present; I return to
> the cyclic time of primitive man. I relive the myth
> of paradise. The real present loses its urgency for
> me, its hold on my responsibility. Nothing has to be
> accomplished, conquered or timed.[32]

Christian worship needs to break people out of this toxic
existentialism by including a sense of where we have come
from. The current interest in the Jewish roots of the
Christian faith, and in Celtic Christian spirituality, are
signs of a growing hunger for a sense of the past. At the
same time, the growing interest in eschatology signals a
new hunger for a sense of the future. We need to work
on ways of teaching people the story of the Church's
journey through time. The challenge is to introduce a
sense of history into worship without bowing down to
the idols of empty traditionalism and false apocalypticism.

Fifthly, Christian worship needs to arise out of a community in which there is true commitment – commitment

to Jesus Christ, and commitment to each other. A small community of say 30, among whom there is a genuine devotion to the Lord and to the fellowship, is of far greater value than a church of 300 among whom there is little commitment to either. A true community will be a community where the relationships are real and, consequently, where God is real too. This is because our sense of the reality of the Lord in our worship is directly related to the level of reality in our relationships with each other. The more real we are with each other, the more real God is to us. The differences between an addicted Church and a healed Church (one in which there are real relationships) look like this:

ADDICTED CHURCH	HEALED CHURCH
People deny sin and hurts	People accept both
People go it alone	People embrace community
Faith in behaviour	Faith in Jesus
A sense of aimlessness	A sense of purpose
Unhealedness remains	The Holy Spirit heals
Manipulation abounds	Honesty abounds
There is never enough	God is all-sufficient
Struggle	Serenity
Tension	Shalom
Introspection	Cheerful outreach
Denial	Reality
Removal of pain	Acceptance of suffering

Authentic worship arises out of authentic community!

The story of Bill Wilson

I have indicated in this chapter that addiction is really the key to understanding our society. Any brave new Church established, by the grace of God, in the run-up to the third millenium must take into account the addictive character of popular culture and of contemporary first-world societies. Anything less would be foolhardy. In the final analysis, the one thing that matters most is *reality*. In an addictive society, what people will find liberating in a brave new Church is its reality – reality in our relationships with ourselves (being honest about who and what we really are), reality in our relationship with others (the freedom to be our real selves), and the reality of the Lord in our worship, both individually and corporately.

The third of these – the reality of the Living God – is worth stressing. People are not primarily looking for doctrine, today: they are looking for reality. The interest in doctrine will follow later. But the thing that will attract unchurched people to church – even the most antagonistic, unchurched atheist! – is an actual encounter with God that is a felt experience. No addiction in the world can compete with that.

Bill Wilson, the founder of Alcoholics Anonymous, was living proof of the truth of that statement. In 1934 he was a loud-mouthed, pompous alcoholic living in New York. He was nearly 40 years old, and feeding his addiction by stealing housekeeping money from his wife's handbag. Eventually he was hospitalised, whereupon a friend called Ebby Thatcher visited him. Ebby had been an alcoholic, but had had such a profound experience of God that he had completely given up. Ebby told Bill, 'Realise you are licked, admit it, and get willing to turn your life to the care of God.'

After Ebby Thatcher left, Bill Wilson struggled with what he had heard. But as the last vestige of pride was crushed, he cried out, 'If there is a God, let him show himself! I am ready to do anything, anything!' Bill Wilson later recorded:

> Suddenly the room lit up with a great white light. I was caught up into an ecstasy which there are no words to describe. It seemed to me, in the mind's eye, that I was on a mountain and that a wind not of air but of spirit was blowing. And then it burst upon me that I was a free man. Slowly the ecstasy subsided. I lay on a bed, but now for a time I was in another world, a new world of consciousness. All about me and through me there was a wonderful feeling of Presence, and I thought to myself, 'So this is the God of the preachers!' A great peace stole over me and I thought, 'No matter how wrong things seem to be, they are all right. Things are all right with God and his world.'

From that day on, Bill Wilson never touched another drop of alcohol.

My conviction is that a brave new Church will indeed emerge in the coming years, and it will emerge from local churches that have opened their doors to the reality of God in this kind of experiential, unmistakable way. When the Holy Spirit comes in power upon a community, that community is intoxicated with the life of God – so much so that some observers mistake it for drunkenness, as at Pentecost. When this happens, often unchurched people forsake the pubs and find their way into church, where they themselves encounter God. In the Welsh Revival in 1904 this was very common, and indeed the breweries were hard hit as many pubs were emptied. The truth of the matter is that being filled with the Spirit of Jesus is far, far better than being filled with anything else. It is the only thing that truly fills the hole in the soul. A brave new Church will both live that truth incarnationally, and proclaim it compassionately. Only such a Church as this will offer a counter-culture in a nation 'oppressed by pleasure, wealth and care'.

The prayer for the Church today is therefore Paul's prayer for the Church in Ephesus:

> I keep asking that the God of our Lord Jesus Christ, the glorious Father, may give you the Spirit of wisdom and relevation, so that you may know him better. I pray also that the eyes of your heart may be enlightened in order that you may know the hope to which he has called you, the riches of his glorious inheritance in the saints, and his incomparably great power for us who believe. (Eph. 1:17–19)

CONCLUSION

In this book I have used Aldous Huxley's *Brave New World* as a window onto contemporary culture. It seems to me, looking back, that things are both worse and better than Huxley imagined. On the one hand, they are worse. In *Brave New World Revisited*, Huxley pointed out that in his novel there were no whisky, no tobacco, no heroin, and no cocaine. People did not smoke, drink, snort, or inject themselves. Whenever people felt low they would simply swallow a tablet or two of *soma*. The number and the variety of addictions therefore makes today's society, in one sense at least, worse than Huxley's dystopia. On the other hand, things are unquestionably better today than in *Brave New World*. There is still no world order (though there is talk of 'a new world order' in international politics[1]), and society is not yet organised on the basis of eugenics. Huxley's nightmare vision is not exactly paralleled by everyday mainstream culture.

Nor am I naive about the book's defects. Though the content of *Brave New World* is certainly important for our times, the form is flawed. For example, I am still unclear about who is the real protagonist of the novel. Is it Bernard Marx? Or is it John (the noble 'Savage')? Secondly, the plot and characterisation seem ultimately to be subservient to the idea that Huxley is trying to put across: the work as a whole feels like an essay dressed up as a novel. Thirdly, the theme itself contains within it a certain instability. Is it Huxley's intention to satirise an American idea of a future utopia? Or is Huxley attempting to provide a blueprint for an actual utopia? At times it is unclear. Fourthly, the Savage himself sometimes talks 'more rationally than his upbringing among the practitioners of a religion that is half fertility cult and half *Penitente* ferocity would actually warrant' (Huxley's own words[2]). Huxley himself was later to say that the defects of *Brave New World* as a work of art are considerable. That accepted, however, the merit of the novel lies in its content, in its astonishingly accurate prediction of how the future might one day look. The future – a future in which society has become numb through addictions of all kinds – is upon us.

Huxley the man

Brave New World is ultimately flawed, like Huxley the man. Aldous Huxley himself was extremely perceptive about the addictive and idolatrous nature of society. In the earlier part of his writing career this emerged particularly powerfully in his novels. In the later part, Huxley turned more to essay writing – which was ultimately his real gift. In spite of all his words about idolatry in society, however, Huxley could never renounce idolatry in his own life. In the latter stages of his life he turned to drugs as a means of coping with reality. His book, *The Doors of Perception*, describes the famous bright May morning on which he took four-tenths of a gram of mescaline dissolved in water.

> I took my pill at eleven. An hour and half later I was sitting in my study, looking intently at a small

glass vase. The vase contained only three flowers –
a full-blown Belle of Portugal rose, shell pink with a
hint at every petal's base of a hotter, flamier hue;
a large magenta and cream-coloured carnation; and,
pale purple at the end of its broken stalk, the bold
heraldic blossom of an iris. Fortuitous and pro-
visional, the little nosegay broke all the rules of
traditional good taste. At breakfast that morning I
had been struck by the lively dissonance of its
colours. But that was no longer the point. I was not
looking now at an unusual flower arrangement. I
was seeing what Adam had seen on the morning of
his creation – the miracle, moment by moment,
of naked existence.[3]

Huxley recommended mescaline as a means of relieving
and consoling our suffering species 'without doing more
harm in the long run than it does good in the short'.[4]
Not long afterwards, particularly as a result of his associ-
ation with Timothy Leary, the interest in mescaline was
developed into an interest in LSD. Alongside this drug
habit, Huxley also developed an interest in Eastern mysticism. These two aspects of his life may not seem to have
much in common, but in reality Huxley used both for
the same purpose – as a means of himself taking holidays
from reality. In *The Doors of Perception*, Huxley gives the
following rationale for his constant attempts at self-trans-
cendence through drugs and mysticism:

That humanity at large will ever be able to dispense
with Artificial Paradises seems very unlikely. Most
men and women lead lives at the worst so painful,
at the best so monotonous, poor and limited that the
urge to escape, the longing to transcend themselves if

only for a few moments, is and has always been one
of the principal appetites of the soul.[5]

Huxley towards the end of his life was advocating a combination of drugs and mysticism as the most effective
means of self-transendence. In his last novel, *Island*,
Huxley attempted to describe another utopia, this time
the island of Pala. Here the people remain in a state of
perpetual happiness through *maithuna* (the yoga of love)
and *moksha* (a hallucinogenic toadstool) – the marriage of
Eastern mysticism and drugs.

Huxley, then, was flawed as a man: though he spent
much of his time renouncing idolatry in society, he lived
a life of idolatry himself. For all his pronouncements
against worshipping addictive objects, relationships and
systems, in the final analysis Huxley himself could not
take his own advice. There was, I believe, a gaping hold
in Huxley's soul – a cavity of pain from the very earliest
days of his life. Maybe it was that year spent in almost
total blindness as a child, a year that must have been
terrifying and confusing for one so young. It could have
been anything. But whatever the pain within, Huxley
himself found that the only way to deal with it was
by resorting to the highs of mystical and drug-induced
experience. Only the temporary euphoria of these false
gods, in the end, was enough. And when Huxley came
to face the greatest fear, the fact of his own death, the
only way he could do so was by resorting to LSD. The
last words he wrote were on a note to his second wife,
Laura: '100 micrograms of LSD. Try it.' The drug was
administered and he died, according to Laura, with a
beatific smile on his face.

Mescaline and mysticism

Aldous Huxley is therefore an imperfect paradigm. Indeed, *The Doors of Perception* – with its open encouragement of drug-taking – was used almost as a kind of textbook in the psychedelic sixties. Yet although we should not be overly romantic about Huxley the man, Huxley the writer is someone special. Throughout his works there are flashes of insight which are increasingly pertinent to us. Witness, for example, the following quotation from *Brave New World Revisited*:

> Religion, Karl Marx declared, is the opium of the people. In the Brave New World this situation was reversed. Opium, or rather *soma*, was the people's religion.[6]

In our own society, opium has become the religion of the people. We have become idolaters of feeling, seeking ecstasy in all the wrong places. Two particularly strong attractions are the very ones Huxley himself advocated, mysticism and drugs. As far as the first is concerned, we may note the tremendous popularity of New Age spiritualities today. One of the reasons for this, according to some experts, is that many New Age groups have the capacity to induce profound personality changes in their adherents. Groups devoted to Eastern religions, paganism, witchcraft and self-awareness therapy are all capable of inducing changes in the brain as intense as those caused by LSD or cannabis. Devotees, in other words, can get high.

As far as the second is concerned, we may note the growing sense of defeatism in the police force concerning illicit drugs. The police have confessed to the public that they have all but given up trying to win the war against cannabis. The problem of addiction to crack, LSD, heroin, ecstasy and other drugs is reaching epidemic proportions. At the same time there is a movement, growing in momentum, that is advocating the legalising of drugs such as cannabis – a movement which has even won the backing of Christian GPs like Peter May. Alongside this, people are resorting more and more to prescription drugs – especially antidepressants and tranquillisers – to cope with the pain and pressures of modern life. Amongst the most significant of these, as I showed in Chapter 2, is the quick-fix wonder drug, Prozac.

The pursuit of happiness

At the root of all this seeking is the need for happiness. The 'pursuit of happiness' is very high on the agenda of first-world societies: it has been since it was explicitly mentioned in the American Bill of Rights, and it has been implicit in Enlightenment consumerist philosophy.

One of the great tasks of the Church in this generation is to engage philosophically and theologically with the pursuit of happiness. Paul himself, in Acts 17:16–34, debated with Epicureans in the marketplace of Athens, and the Epicureans were the classic exponents of hedonism – the pursuit of happiness and pleasure. We need likewise to debate with the latter-day Epicureans of our own culture. We need to remind them of the hedonistic paradox, which goes as follows:

> If you seek pleasure but fail to find it, you will be miserable in your frustration. If you seek pleasure and you do find it, you will soon become bored, and

you will in fact be as miserable as you would have been had you failed in your search.

Huxley himself was aware of this paradox. In his essay, 'Religion and time', he wrote:

> Happiness is not achieved by the conscious pursuit of happiness; it is generally the by-product of other activities. This 'hedonistic paradox' may be generalized to cover our whole life in time.[7]

That is very true. For Christians, the greatest happiness is the service of God, which is, paradoxically, our greatest freedom. True healing and salvation come through following Jesus Christ. After that, true happiness comes as a by-product of seeking first the kingdom of God and his righteousness (Matt. 6:33). As we seek first God's agenda for our lives, all the other things that the world depends upon will be added unto us – clothes to wear, food to eat, things to drink, money enough to be content (Matt. 6:25–34). Furthermore, as we worship the Father through Jesus the Son, the Holy Spirit touches and fills us with a sense of Divine Presence that brings far more joy than any temporary anaesthesia induced by addictions. True happiness – 'solid joys and lasting pleasures' – is felt as a by-product of costly discipleship. It is not found by seeking happiness as an end in itself.

Holy indifference

If there is one practical application from this book, it has to do with what Huxley (in an essay title) called 'Mortification, non-attachment, right livelihood'. In that essay, Huxley reminds us that:

The divine eternal fullness of life can be gained
only by those who have deliberately lost the partial,
separative life of craving and self-interest, of egocen-
tric thinking, feeling, wishing and acting.[8]

The key thing is therefore to start living a life of holy
indifference to the addictive objects, ideas, relationships
and behaviours we have adopted. As Huxley warned,

Until we put an end to our particular attachments,
there can be no love of God with the whole heart,
mind and strength and no universal charity towards
all creatures for God's sake.[9]

Or, as he put in more poetically in 'Man and reality',

We cannot see the moon and the stars so long as we
choose to remain within the aura of street lamps and
whisky advertisements.[10]

In the final analysis, Huxley's writings are a constant
reminder of the oppressive nature of our age. In an essay
entitled 'Distractions', Huxley demonstrated that ours is
an age in which everyone is in love with aimless stimulation:

Men have always been a prey to distractions, which
are the original sin of the mind; but never before
today has an attempt been made to organize and
exploit distractions, to make of them, because of
their economic importance, the core and vital centre
of human life, to idealize them as the highest mani-
festations of mental activity.[11]

'Ours', writes Huxley, 'is an age of systemized irrel-
evances', and many have allowed themselves to be enslaved
by triviality and amusement. But there is a better way

of life. A life of complete trust in the Father, a life of detachment modelled on the person of Jesus, a life of being filled with the Holy Spirit rather than any man-made anaesthetic – that is the better way. That is the way of freedom: for where the Spirit of the Lord is, there is freedom. Indeed, the Spirit is, supremely, *Spiritus Liberator*, the Spirit who leads the oppressed people of God on their exodus out of slavery.

In *Brave New World*, John the Savage asks the people, 'Don't you want to be free?' That seems to me to be the question asked from heaven in our generation,

'My children, don't you want to be free?'

Appendix 1:
Living a kingdom lifestyle in an addictive society
Notes for small groups

Session 1: Matthew 6:1-4

Background

Matthew 6:1–4 introduces one of three secret acts of righteousness which are to characterise every Christian disciple.

What are these three acts of righteousness (see vv.1–4, vv.5–15, vv.16–18)? Are these three acts an optional extra for super-spiritual people? Or are they the irreducible minimum of the Christian's lifestyle – the basics?

Study

v.1   - What do you think Jesus meant by 'acts of righteousness'?
      - Why do Christians have to be righteous people?
      - What kind of rewards does the Father give to the righteous?
v.2   - What does the word 'hypocrite' mean?
      - Why are churchgoers accused of hypocrisy?
      - Is this charge justified?
      - What reward have hypocrites received (past tense)?
      - What is the full sense of the word 'giving'?

- What does that tell you?
- How important is financial giving in the Christian life?
- Who are the needy?
- Are you giving at the right level now?
- Is there any way you as a group could give in some corporate way to the needy?

v.3 - What do you think Jesus is saying here?
v.4 - Why is secrecy so important?
- Do we help people to be secret in their giving?
- What would your Father say about your secret history of righteous acts thus far?
- What would your Father say about your secret history of unrighteous acts thus far?
- What have you heard God saying to *you* through this passage of Scripture?
- What steps are you going to take this week to change?

Session 2: Matthew 6:5–15

Background

In the last session you looked at the first of our three daily acts of righteousness, namely 'giving'. Today you look at the second of these, 'prayer'.

What is prayer? Why is it so essential? How well are you doing individually and as a group in the practice of prayer?

Study

v.5 - Have you ever witnessed this kind of hypocrisy?
- Are you ever guilty of ostentatious prayer?

        – What does this verse have to say about prayer
          marches?

v.6   – The word translated 'room' is the Greek word
          for the secret treasure chamber at the heart of a
          Palestinian home. Have you a secret place like
          this for prayer? How easy do you find it to
          get privacy for prayer? Is your place of prayer
          somewhere in which you find spiritual treasures?
          What are you going to do to find such a place?

v.7   – What did Jesus mean by 'babbling'? Do you ever
          'babble' in prayer? What does this verse tell you
          about long prayers? What kinds of religious
          jargon make our prayers long and 'babbly'?

v.8   – If the Father knows what we need before we
          pray, why pray?

v.9   – Jesus says this is 'how' you should pray, not 'what'
          you should pray. What does this suggest to you
          about the way Jesus intended this prayer to be
          used?

        – This prayer is often called 'the family prayer'. Is
          that a helpful description? What is so important
          about the way the prayer opens? Do you find it
          difficult to address God as 'Father'?

v.10 – What is meant by 'kingdom'? Do you want to
          see the kingdom come in your area?

v.11 – Do you find it difficult to pray for your own
          needs?

v.12 – Can you really say the second part of this verse
          and mean it?

v.13 – How much is 'warfare prayer' a part of your
          prayer life?

v.14 – Do you find it difficult to forgive others?
        – What happens if you don't forgive them?

- Should you ever go and forgive someone to her or his face?
- What lifestyle changes have you made since the group last met? What lifestyles changes are you going to make now?

Session 3: Matthew 6:16–18

Background

Fasting is a secret act of righteousness. It is a spiritual discipline which we are encouraged to do. Like giving and praying, fasting is not an optional extra for the super-spiritual but a basic fact (part of the irreducible minimum) of the Christian life. How does that make you feel?

Study

v.16
- Notice that Jesus does not say 'if you fast' but rather 'when you fast'. What does that tell you?
- What is 'fasting'?
- Why should Christians fast?
- What are the benefits of fasting?
- How often should a Christian fast?
- Are there other things besides food from which you should fast?
- Are there special seasons or times for fasting?
- What should your motives be for fasting?

v.17
- What is Jesus warning us about here?
- What would be contemporary equivalents of oil on the head and the washing of faces?
- Why bother with such things?
- If the physical effects of fasting are so obvious,

what does this tell you about fasting as a
discipline?

v.18 - What are the rewards of fasting?
      - What truths have you learnt from this passage of
        Scripture?
      - How are you getting on in relation to this par-
        ticular act of righteousness?
      - Is there anything you can do as a group to help
        one another in the discipline of fasting?
      - How are you getting on with the other two acts
        of righteousness?

Session 4: Matthew 6:19–24

Background

We move now from the three acts of righteousness to a
new block of material (6:19–34). In 6:1–18 Jesus describes
the Christian's *private* life in 'the secret place' (giving,
praying, fasting). In 6:19–34 Jesus is concerned with our
public business in the world (questions of money, pos-
sessions, food, drink, clothing, ambition). Every aspect of
our lives must therefore come under the Spirit's scrutiny.

Study

v.19 - What did Jesus mean by 'earthly treasures'? What
        are the treasures that you tend to prize?
      - What did he mean by 'storing up'?
      - Why is the accumulation of wealth so pointless?
      - Why do people store up material things?
      - Is there anything that you are storing up?
v.20 - What are 'treasures in heaven'?
      - How do you store these?

- Why do you store them?
v.21 - How important to God is your heart?
- What is your heart after at the moment?
- Is your passion a holy passion for the things of God?
v.22 - What does Jesus mean in these two verses?
- How would you get on at a 'spiritual optician'?
v.23 - What are some of the things that you see that pollute your heart?
- How easy is it to avoid them?
- What steps practically could you take to keep your eyes pure?
v.24 - Do Christians try to serve two masters?
- How can you break the idolatry of materialism in your area?
- Is it possible to be a rich Christian?
- What changes could you make to become anti-materialistic?

Session 5: Matthew 6:25–34

Introduction

You may be thinking by now that this study material is a bit dogmatic, a bit black and white. Well, that's because Jesus' teaching is, too! John Stott, in his commentary on this text, says, 'Jesus places the alternatives before us at every stage. There are two treasures (on earth and in heaven, 19–21), two bodily conditions (light and darkness, 22, 23), two masters (God and mammon, 24) and two preoccupations (our bodies and God's kingdom, 25–34)'. In today's session we are going to look at what Jesus says about 'worry' in verses 25–34 of this chapter.

Study

v.25   - Why does Jesus start this verse with the word 'therefore'?
- What is 'worry'?
- What sort of things do we worry about?
- What are the things Jesus identifies as causes of worry?
- Why do we worry about these and other things?
- How easy is it to obey the command, 'Do not worry'?
- Should Christians ever worry?

v.27   - Is worrying healthy?
- Is worrying addictive?

v.30   - What does Jesus put 'worry' down to in Christians?
- What does Jesus mean by 'faith'?

v.34   - How much time do we spend worrying about the future?
- What kinds of things in the future do we worry about?
- How many times does Jesus say 'Don't worry?'
- What strategies can you devise to deal with worry?
- How can you help one another as a group in the matter of worry?

Session 6: Matthew 6:25–34

Introduction

One of the main themes of this passage is 'worry', and you looked at that subject in the last session. Today you look at another theme of the passage, 'eating'.

Isn't it interesting that Jesus addresses all aspects of our lives? That he's interested in us developing a kingdom perspective on matters as basic as 'eating'? Begin the session by discussing whether you have a Christian perspective on eating habits. Do any of you have a Christian philosophy of food and eating?

Study

v.25   - Jesus commands us not to worry about what we're going to eat. How relevant is that in a rich country like ours?
      - How relevant is this in third-world countries?
      - Are people addicted to food and to eating?
      - If so, why? What is at the root of overeating?

v.26   - What can we learn about God from Jesus' words here?
      - What does the warning against 'storing' teach us?

v.31   - Do you ever worry about where the next meal is coming from?
      - What single spiritual quality do we need to cultivate in order to stop worrying?
      - What barriers are there in us that prevent us from enjoying this quality?
      - Can 'worry' become an addiction?

Session 7: Matthew 6:25–34

Introduction

Last week we looked at eating; today we look at drinking. Jesus addresses this subject in verses 25 and 31. Look at those verses together and discuss them.

In this session, look specifically at the consumption of alcohol. The verses in Matthew 6 refer to drinking habits in general, but concentrate on the consumption of alcohol, as it is such a problem today. What is it about our society that makes people seek after anaesthetics such as alcohol?

Study

- Look up Ephesians 5:18. This is part of a holiness code extending from 4:17 to 6:20. These commands are issued to Christians, not to non-Christians.
- Paul says, 'Do not get drunk on wine.' Is he saying 'Don't drink wine at all'? (Compare 1 Timothy 5:23.)
- What are the destructive consequences of getting drunk? (Look up Proverbs 23:29–35.)
- What kind of person gets high on beer and wine, according to Proverbs 20:1?
- Why do people drink alcohol in quantity, according to Proverbs 31:6–7?
- What are the sorts of things that people are trying to forget when they drink too much?
- Returning to Ephesians 5:18, Paul says that getting drunk on wine leads to debauchery. What does he mean by 'debauchery'?
- What alternative does Paul suggest, in Ephesians 5:18?
- What does it mean to be 'filled with the Spirit'?
- Why is this a healthy alternative to drunkenness?
- Can you spot any parallels with Acts 2:13?
- How do we get filled with the Spirit? (See Luke 11:11–13.)
- What kinds of behaviour does the fullness of the Spirit produce? (See Ephesians 5:19–20.)

- What boundaries should we therefore set to our drinking of alcohol?
- How many units of alcohol can men and women imbibe each week to remain within a healthy limit?

Session 8: Matthew 6:25–34

Introduction

The third specific 'worry' that Jesus addresses in these verses is 'clothes'. Just as food addiction and alcohol addiction are common in our culture, so also is 'clothes' addiction.

In groups of three, go through a weekend colour supplement. Cut out everything that promotes these addictions. Discuss together what you have found.

Now read verses 28–33 of Matthew 6.

Study

v.28 - Why *do* people worry about clothes?
- How preoccupied are you with dress sense?
- Why do nice clothes matter to you?
- Is it right to look untidy?
- How concerned about your image should you be?
- How does society feed the need to look good?
- What is society's definition of 'looking good', for both men and women?
- How does that make people feel if they cannot look that way?
- Why does Jesus admire the lilies?
- Is this a literal prohibition against making clothes?

v.29   - What does this verse tell you about Jesus' idea
         of dress sense?
       - How does it differ from cultural norms?
v.30   - Will God meet our basic needs, such as the need
         for clothes?
       - What priorities must we have if God is going to
         provide our needs? (See Matthew 6:33.)
v.32   - What does it mean to 'run after' food, drink,
         clothes?
       - To what extent is our contemporary culture
         manifesting pagan characteristics?

Session 9: Matthew 6:25–34

Introduction

We have now done an exhaustive study of Matthew,
Chapter 6. It has taken a long time to unearth the heav-
enly treasures of just one chapter of the Bible (see
Matthew 6:20)! Think how many treasures there are in a
biblical book!

In this final session, review the notes for the eight
previous sessions. Spend some time speaking to someone
else about what lifestyle changes you have made, and what
lessons you have learnt.

Then, as a group, construct a kind of monastic 'rule of
life'. Such a rule consists of a list of values and intentions.
These are not laws to be obeyed, but a basis for seeking
to live a truly kingdom lifestyle (Matthew 6:33).

Now construct a list of kingdom values for the following subjects, discussed in Matthew 6. Begin each point
with the following phrase, 'We recommend that . . .'

   1. Giving.

2. Prayer.
3. Fasting.
4. Money.
5. Worry.
6. Eating.
7. Drinking.
8. Clothes.

Conclusion

How prepared are you to live out these values as a small-group community? What practical steps are you going to take to become a Christian counter-culture in an addictive society?

Have a look at the Twelve-Step programme employed by small groups in Alcoholics Anonymous and related organisations. What can you learn from this? How can you live it out?

Spend some time praying for one another, if appropriate for release from addictions (with the laying on of hands).

Commission one another to live out a righteous kingdom lifestyle.

Ask someone to write up your community rule, and to give a copy to each member of the group. Come back to the rule at a future date, to see how you're all doing!

Appendix 2:
The works of Aldous Huxley

Novels

Crome Yellow
Antic Hay
Those Barren Leaves
Point Counter Point
Brave New World
Eyeless in Gaza
After Many a Summer
Time Must Have a Stop
Ape and Essence
The Genius and the Goddess
Island

Short stories

Limbo
Mortal Coils
Little Mexican
Two or Three Graces
Brief Candles
The Gioconda Smile (Collected short stories)

Biography

Grey Eminence
The Devils of Loudun

Travel

Along the Road
Jesting Pilate
Beyond the Mexique Bay

Poetry and drama

The Burning Wheel
Jonah
The Defeat of Youth
Leda
Verses and a Comedy
The Gioconda Smile

Essays and belles lettres

On the Margin
Proper Studies
Do What You Will
Music at Night
Texts and Pretexts
The Olive Tree
Ends and Means
The Art of Seeing
The Perennial Philosophy

Science, Liberty and Peace
Themes and Variations
The Doors of Perception
Adonis and the Alphabet
Heaven and Hell
Brave New World Revisited
Literature and Science
The Human Situation
Moksha

For children

The Crows of Pearblossom

All of these were republished by Flamingo in special, paperback, centenary editions.

Notes

Introduction

1. William Langley, 'Pizza de Résistance', *The Sunday Times* ('Style' section), 25 September 1994.
2. Walter Brueggemann, *The Prophetic Imagination* (London, SCM, 1992; first published 1978), p. 13.
3. Stan Wilson, *Mass Media/Mass Culture* (New York, McGraw-Hill, 1993 updated edition), pp. 4–5.
4. Aldous Huxley, *Brave New World* (London, Marshall Cavendish, 1988), p. 105. [The 'Great Writers Library' edition: hereafter *BNW*.]

Chapter 1: 'O brave new world!'

1. Huxley, *BNW,* p. 115.
2. Neil Postman, *Amusing Ourselves to Death: Public Discourse in the Age of Show Business* (London, Heinemann, 1986), p. vii.
3. ibid. p. vii.
4. ibid. p. vii.
5. Huxley, *BNW,* p. 1.
6. ibid. p. 21.
7. ibid. p. 183.
8. ibid. p. 47.
9. ibid. p. 163.
10. ibid. p. 54.
11. ibid. p. 128.
12. ibid. p. 125.
13. ibid. p. 200.
14. Huxley, *BNW,* 1946 Foreword.
15. ibid.

16. Aldous Huxley, *Brave New World Revisited* (London, Harper Collins, 1983), p. 11. [Hereafter *BNWR.*]
17. ibid, p. 12.
18. Huxley, *BNW,* 1946 Foreword.
19. ibid.
20. Huxley, *BNWR,* p. 47.
21. Postman, *Amusing Ourselves to Death,* p. 155.

Chapter 2: Our social destiny

1. Huxley, *BNW,* p. 28.
2. Editorial comment, *The Daily Telegraph,* 16 August 1993.
3. Neville Hodgkinson, 'The master race', *The Sunday Times* ('Focus' section), 2 January 1994.
4. *The Sunday Times,* 9 February 1992.
5. Huxley, *BNW,* p. 18.
6. The visuals and the data for this section are taken from Charles Murray, 'Underclass: the crisis deepens', *The Sunday Times* ('Focus' section), 22 May 1994.
7. ibid. p. 10.
8. ibid. p. 11.
9. ibid. p. 11.
10. Huxley, *BNW,* p. 32.
11. Huxley, *BNWR,* pp. 84–5.
12. ibid. p. 89.
13. Wilson, *Mass Media/Mass Culture,* p. 304.
14. ibid. p. 317.
15. ibid. p. 323.
16. ibid. p. 322.
17. Oliver James and Sue Clarke, 'The feel-good factor', *The Sunday Times* ('Style & Travel' supplement), 18 July 1993.
18. Peter Kramer, *Listening to Prozac* (London, Fourth Estate, 1993).
19. James and Clarke, 'Feel-good factor'.
20. Quoted in James and Clarke, 'Feel-good factor'.
21. James and Clarke, 'Feel-good-factor'.

Chapter 3: No leisure from pleasure

1. Huxley, *BNW*, p. 12.
2. ibid. p. 23.
3. ibid. p. 24.
4. From the song 'The Right Thing' on the album *Men and Women*, WEA Records Ltd, 1987.
5. Michael Medved, *Hollywood Versus America: Popular Culture and the War on Traditional Values* (New York, Harper Collins, 1992), pp. 95–100.
6. The material which follows is based on the article, 'Sex in the movies', *Empire* magazine, May 1993, pp. 76–85.
7. ibid.
8. Huxley, *BNW*, p. 137.
9. ibid. p. 137.
10. Quoted from the opening sequence of the video release of *The Lawnmower Man*.
11. Barrie Sherman and Phil Judkins, *Glimpses of Heaven, Visions of Hell: Virtual Reality and its Implications* (London, Hodder & Stoughton, 1992).
12. ibid. p. 191.
13. ibid. p. 114.
14. ibid. p. 192.
15. Huxley, *BNW*, p. 63.
16. ibid. pp. 65–71.
17. ibid. p. 67.
18. ibid. p. 67.
19. ibid. p. 70.
20. Aldous Huxley, *The Doors of Perception* (London, Flamingo, 1994, p. 7. [Hereafter *DP*.]
21. ibid. p. 1.
22. Huxley, *BNW*, p. 68.
23. Quoted in Imogen Edwards-Jones, 'Weld music', *The Sunday Times* ('Style & Travel' section), 12 December 1993.
24. Quoted in Fiona Lafferty, 'Ecstasy?', *The Sunday Times* ('Style & Travel' section), 1994.
25. ibid.
26. Aldous Huxley, *Huxley and God: Essays*, edited by Jacqueline

Hazard Bridgeman (San Francisco, Harper Collins, 1992),
pp. 121–2. [Hereafter *HGE*.]

Chapter 4: Christianity without tears

1. Huxley, *BNW,* p. 195.
2. Anne Wilson Schaef, *When Society Becomes an Addict* (San Francisco, HarperCollins, 1988). [Hereafter *WSBA*.]
3. Howard Clinebell, 'Philosophical-religious factors in the etiology and treatment of alcoholism', *Quarterly Journal of Studies on Alcohol* 24 (1963), pp. 473–88.
4. Rebecca Gardiner, 'Addicted to sex', *Options*, March 1992.
5. ibid. p. 38.
6. ibid. p. 38.
7. ibid. p. 39.
8. ibid. p. 39.
9. Robert Hemfelt and Richard Fowler, *Serenity: A Companion for Twelve Step Recovery, Complete with New Testament, Psalms & Proverbs* (Nashville, Thomas Nelson, 1990), pp. 13–14.
10. The graphic is by Paddy Allen, and is from *Educational Guardian*, 12 November 1991.
11. Larry Collins, 'The seeds of misery', *The Sunday Times News Review,* 14 November 1993.
12. Lafferty, 'Ecstasy?'
13. Charles Hymas, 'Schoolchildren risk health with heavy drinking', *The Sunday Times*, 10 January 1993.
14. Schaef, *WSBA*, p. 22.
15. Fiona Webster, 'The crime of their lives', *The Sunday Times* ('Style & Travel' section), 23 June 1993.
16. Beatrix Campbell, *Goliath: Britain's Dangerous Places* (London, Methuen, 1993).
17. Marcus Brill, 'Enter the Cyberdude', *The Sunday Times* ('Style & Travel' section), 24 April 1994.
18. Huxley, *HGE*, p. 168.
19. Anne Wilson Schaef, *Escape from Intimacy: Untangling the 'Love' Addictions: Sex, Romance, Relationships* (New York, Harper Collins, 1992).
20. ibid. p. 3.

21. ibid. p. 33.
22. Lori Rentzel, *Emotional Dependency* (Exodus International Book-let, 1987), pp. 3–4.
23. Susan Forward, *Obsessive Love: When Passion Holds you Prisoner* (New York, Bantam, 1991), p. 8.
24. Mike Featherstone, *Consumer Culture and Postmodernism* (London, Sage, 1991).
25. ibid. p. 27.
26. Huxley, *BNWR*, p. 113.
27. Cited in Ilana Belle Glass (ed.), *The International Handbook of Addiction Behaviour* (London & New York, Routledge, 1991), pp. 26–7.
28. Huxley, *BNWR*, p. 61.

Chapter 5: Brave new Church

1. Huxley, *BNW,* p. 194.
2. Huxley, *DP,* p. 47.
3. ibid. p. 46.
4. ibid. p. 48.
5. See Martin Helldorfer, 'Church professionals and work addiction', *Studies in Formative Spirituality,* VIII, pt. 2 (1987), pp. 199–210. [Hereafter *SFS.*]
6. See Patrick Carnes, 'Sexual addiction: implications for spiritual formation', *SFS,* pp. 165–74.
7. James Royce, 'Alcohol and other drugs in spiritual formation', *SFS,* p. 211.
8. ibid.
9. Grant Martin, *Regaining Control: When Good Things Become Addictions* (Washington, Victor Books, 1990), pp. 133–4.
10. Schaef, *WSBA,* pp. 37–95.
11. ibid. pp. 37–8.
12. ibid. p. 41.
13. ibid. p. 50.
14. ibid. p. 66.
15. ibid. p. 68.
16. ibid. p. 78.
17. Carnes, 'Sexual addiction', p. 168.

18. Royce, 'Alcohol and other drugs', pp. 214–15.
19. Schaef, *WSBA*, p. 37.
20. Royce, 'Alcohol and other drugs', p. 215.
21. Huxley, *HGE*, pp. 20–1.
22. ibid. p. 121.
23. ibid. p. 129.
24. ibid. p. 170.
25. ibid. p. 46.
26. Cited in Vic Ramsay, *Addiction & The Vitamin Factor: An Answer to Dependency* (Basingstoke, Marshall Pickering, 1986), pp. 69–70.
27. Cited in *The Sunday Times Magazine*, 16 October 1994.
28. Howard Rheingold, *The Virtual Community: Finding Connection in a Computerised World* (Secker, 1993).
29. David Watson, *Discipleship* (London, Hodder & Stoughton, 1989), p. 52.
30. Clinebell, 'Philosophical-religious factors', pp. 479–80.
31. Aldous Huxley, *The Perennial Philosophy* (London, Flamingo, 1994), p. 310. From his essay, 'Emotionalism'.
32. Adrian Van Kaam, *SFS*, p. 252.

Conclusion

1. For an interesting study of the way in which 'a new world order' is emerging in international politics, and its uncanny and disturbing similarities to what Huxley envisaged in *BNW*, see Jack Nelson Pallmeyer, *Brave New World Order: Must We Pledge Allegiance?* (New York, Orbis, 1992).
2. Huxley, *BNW*, 1946 Foreword.
3. Huxley, *DP*, p. 7.
4. ibid. p. 44.
5. ibid. p. 42.
6. Huxley, *BNWR*, pp. 114–15.
7. Huxley, *HGE*, p. 75.
8. Huxley, *The Perennial Philosophy*, p. 114.
9. ibid. p. 123.
10. Huxley, *HGE*, p. 93.
11. ibid. p. 157.